GO!

The excitem

GW00384627

GO!

The excitement of personal
evangelism

DANNY LEHMANN

HODDER & STOUGHTON
LONDON SYDNEY AUCKLAND TORONTO

British Library Cataloguing in Publication Data

Lehmann, Danny
  Go!: the excitement of personal evangelism
  – (Hodder Christian paperbacks).
  1. Witness bearing (Christianity)
  I. Title
  248'.5   BV4520

  ISBN 0-340-42591-1

Contents

Chapter 1

Needed – a volunteer army

"Your troops will be willing on your day of battle. Arrayed in holy majesty, from the womb of the dawn you will receive the dew of your youth." (Psalm 110:3)

Evangelism is the first priority of the church. Such a statement may seem radical and extreme to some, but it should help us see the urgency of the task our Lord has laid before us. From the jungles of Papua New Guinea to the streets of Amsterdam and Beverly Hills there are men and women who are eternally lost, living in spiritual darkness and alienated from God. As we go on in this book we will see that Scripture plainly teaches they will stay that way unless someone cares enough for them to go and lead them to the Light.

One of the most tragic phrases uttered in the Bible is found in Psalm 142:4 where the Psalmist declares ". . . no man is concerned for me." This question should be on the lips of every potential evangelist – DO I CARE? Do I care about, and love, those who are dying every day without Christ? If you do care, or if you want to start caring, then I trust this book will help you in developing a caring *lifestyle* of evangelism. Success in evangelism depends not so much on talent and ability, but on whether or not we really care. Both Jesus and Paul told us that love should be the bottom line of everything we do in the

Christian life, and this is nowhere more true than when it comes to evangelism.

This book is written out of a sense of urgency and hope. Urgency, because despite the headway the gospel is making around the world, the church continues to grow at a slower pace than the population. Urgency, because while sin continues on unchecked in our world it causes incredible pain and suffering. But, most of all, urgency because God's heart breaks every time another soul slips into a Christless eternity. It is written also in the hope that the people of God will take the Great Commission seriously, mobilise and see the task completed. It is the hope that springs from faith in a God who wants the job done, and that the kingdoms of this world will eventually become the kingdoms of our Lord and of his Christ (Rev. 11:15).

This book is also written with one purpose in mind, that of recruiting and equipping volunteers for God's army who will, in turn, commit themselves to finishing the task Jesus has given us (John 4:34). It is geared for both the Christian in the nine-to-five working world, and the prospective missionary candidate. While not all of us are called to be cross-cultural evangelists, we are all called to be witnesses, and in this book we will examine the motives, message and methods that a witness must have and use. We will examine them in the light of God's Word, our final authority.

The apostle Paul did not see evangelism as the job of slick professionals, but as the work of every Christian called of God (Eph. 4:11–13). He did not have a department store mentality when it came to evangelism. In his life evangelism was not stuffed into a corner, like a department in a shop, and occasionally visited when it was "outreach time". Paul tells us that he did all things for the sake of the gospel, that his whole life was committed to spreading the good news (1 Cor. 9:20–3). He had developed a "lifestyle" of evangelism, so that, whether preaching on Mars Hill, discipling Timothy, planting churches, or making tents, his life was consumed with his relationship to Jesus and the task he had given him – "To preach to the Gentiles the unsearchable riches of Christ" (Eph. 3:8).

There is a temptation to relegate this type of lifestyle to spiritual giants, or super-Christians, like Paul. "Yes, well that's fine for him, he was an apostle. I'm not." Paul was aware he would be put on a pedestal, so took pains to show he was just the same as every other Christian, even going so far as to call himself the "worst of sinners" (1 Tim. 1:15). While he made it clear that not all are called to be apostles, he exhorted us to imitate his lifestyle (1 Cor. 11:1; 12:1–31; Phil. 3:17; 4:9). The main thrust of Paul's teaching was that all Christians are called to be functioning parts of the Body, working together to see that it multiplies and grows (Eph. 4:16).

Romans 10:14 makes the nature of evangelism very clear. Paul tells us that people cannot be saved unless they hear the word, so we must preach it! For many of us such a command is frightening, but it need not be. There are three Greek words used in the New Testament, in relation to spreading the gospel, but only one of them, *kerusso* – to proclaim like a herald – has to do with street corner preaching. The other two, *euggeizoai* – to tell good news, and *martureo* – to bear witness, simply mean to share the gospel and bear witness to the truth by whatever means we can. Michael Green said, "When men have the will to speak of their Lord they find no shortage of ways to do it." Many of us do not feel called to street corner preaching, but, as we seek the Lord, he will show us numerous ways we can share his love with the lost (*Evangelism in the Early Church*, p. 278).

Some recent surveys have revealed that up to 90 per cent of Christians in the church today have never led someone to Christ. On the other hand, the American Institute of Church Growth reports that 75 to 90 per cent of believers active in the church today are there because of a personal contact they had with a concerned Christian

(*Christianity Today*, 9 May 1984). Imagine the phenomenal growth there would be in churches if EVERY Christian, not just the 10 per cent, were having personal contact with unbelievers and leading them to Jesus! I believe one of the major items on God's agenda right now is a revival in the area of personal evangelism. There needs to be a renewed emphasis, both from the pulpit, and in the pew, on the responsibility God has placed on all of us to win people for Christ. There need to be evangelists who will take the time to equip believers for evangelism, and pastors who will encourage their congregations to get involved in the task. We need to see godly men and women demonstrate a lifestyle of evangelism, and sound the trumpet of war as they lead us on to the frontlines of evangelism.

We need, however, to be vaccinated against a disease I call "Areopagitus", which had infected the philosophers on Mars Hill (Acts 17:19–21). The main symptom of this disease is a fascination with anything "new". While the tear-filled eyes of a broken-hearted heavenly Father scan the earth for labourers to work in his harvest field, we are busy giving our energy to the latest new sensation that is taking the church by storm, be it Christian diets, dating, self-esteem, mood-control, exercise programmes, or the latest "new" revelation from one of the watchdogs of God's flock. Oh, for a return to the simple holy boldness and fiery zeal that sent the ordinary disciples in the early church "preaching the Word wherever they went" (Acts 8:4).

We live at an exciting point in human history! The prophet Joel and the apostle Peter both spoke of an army that God would raise up in the last days, and upon whom he would pour out his Spirit. This army would use the dreams of the old and the vision and energy of the young to prophesy, or speak forth God's anointed word, to their generation. To his children of the last days, he promised not only the anointing that comes from being Spirit-filled, but also that they would receive a special anointing to proclaim the gospel in the end-times (Acts 2:17–21). While they might not agree on all the particulars, today many believe we are living in that period known as the last days. Across the body of Christ worldwide is the cry that God is preparing his people for a great thrust of evangelism that will reach to every corner of the earth and usher multitudes into the kingdom of God. Just as in any army, success in battle depends on the obedience of each individual soldier to the orders of the commander-in-chief, so in God's army we must be willing and ready to obey those orders that come down to us from our commander-in-chief. Indeed, he has already issued his command – GO!

We live also at a point in history where the need of world evangelism has never been greater, but then, neither has the potential to meet that need been as great as it is today! In 1974 the church reeled as Ralph Winter, speaking at the Lausanne Congress on World Evangelism, laid out the magnitude of the task of world evangelism still to be done. We learned that there were 16,750 distinct ethnic groups, accounting for nearly three billion people who were either culturally, linguistically, socially, or geographically removed from any existing church or mission. Many of these groups are resistant to the gospel, and located in countries where it is nearly impossible to go as a tourist, let alone obtain a missionary visa. Such facts and figures can make us feel depressed and apathetic, but we need to stop being impressed by Satan's dominion in the earth, and start crying out to God for his kingdom to come, and his will to be done on earth as it is in heaven. Our concern should not be over all the closed doors to the gospel, but over making sure that we go through all those doors that are open before it is too late. Samuel Zwemer, a pioneer missionary to the Muslim world, said, "Opportunism is not the last word in missions. The open door beckons; the closed door challenges him who has a right to enter." When we begin to think seriously about world evangelism it seems an impossible task. To establish a church in every one of the 16,750 people groups by the year 2000 would require at least one church per day be established. As well, to reach the nearly three billion people who have never heard the gospel, we would have to reach one new person every second of every day for the next ninety-five years, and that is not accounting for the population growth! It is easy in the light of this to be overawed by Satan's dominion, but we need to be impressed with who God is.

We serve the God of the impossible! Jesus said, "What is impossible with men is possible with God" (Luke 18:27) and, "With God all things are possible" (Matt. 19:26). Again he promises, "Everything is possible for him that believes" (Mark 9:23). We need to be consumed in prayer for the impossible task of world evangelism, praying as if it all depended on God yet working as if it all depends on us. As we respond in this way, God, in his grace, will act and we will see the task completed. All this, however, is dependent on us, his servants, saved by grace, doing all we can to get the job done, which in turn brings pleasure to the heart of God. Just as a father receives joy and responds in love to his son when he does what is asked of him, so too, our heavenly Father receives joy and responds to us when we do what he has asked.

Jesus said, "All authority in heaven and on earth has been given to me" (Matt. 28:18). In other words, he has been given the right to rule over our lives. If we take the terms that Jesus laid down, then like a bond-servant we have given up our rights (Rom. 1:1; Phil. 1:1; James 1:1). He is Lord over our possessions (Luke 14:33), relationships (Luke 14:26; Matt. 10:37), time (Eph. 5:16), money . . . in fact over everything, and he wants our total and absolute surrender. "If Christ be God, and died for me, then no sacrifice I could make would be too great for him," said C. T. Studd, pioneer missionary to Africa. The Lord of the Harvest is calling us as his children to truly seek his kingdom first, and once and for all lay down the right to run our own lives. "You are not your own; you were bought at a price." (1 Cor. 6:19–20). If he has the authority in our lives then he is the one calling the tune, and the last tune he called in the Bible was to "GO and make disciples of all nations . . ." He is calling for an army of volunteers who will commit themselves to a lifetime of love and service for him, the King of Kings. "To know God and make him known" should be our rallying cry as we gather at the cross ready to take on the cause for which he gave his life.

We are often told that we are "King's Kids", and should live like princes. With this I could not agree more, except that there is one thing we must not forget about our king – he is at war! We need to daily remind ourselves of this fact, because as long as our king is at war we are also at war, and so must become soldiers in his army and fight the enemy until that glorious day when "The kingdom of the world has become the kingdom of our Lord and of his Christ" (Rev. 11:15). Our daily habits and lifestyle serve as a visual demonstration to all of how much we really believe we are at war!

WHERE ARE THE RADICALS?

Karl Marx said, "Philosophers have only interpreted the world differently; the point, however, is to change it." All over the world people are working for different causes they feel will make the world a better place. Communism is just one of those causes, and its growth worldwide is in direct relation to the number, and dedication, of its members. In just sixty years this godless philosophy which declares religion to be the opiate of the masses, and this life all there is to live for, has taken over one third of the world. The following is a well-known excerpt from a Communist student's challenge to the church:

The gospel is a much more powerful weapon for the renewal of society than is our Marxist philosophy, but all the same it is we who will finally beat you [. . .] We Communists do not play with words. We are realists, and seeing that we are determined to achieve our object, we know how to obtain the means. Of our salaries and wages we keep only what is strictly necessary, and we give up our free time and part of our holidays. You, however, give only a little time and hardly any money for the spreading of the gospel of Christ. How can anybody believe in the supreme value of this gospel if you do not practise it, if you do not spread it, and if you sacrifice neither time nor money for it . . . ? We believe in our Communist message and we are ready to sacrifice everything, even our life . . . But you people are afraid even to soil your hands. (Quoted in *I Believe in Evangelism* by D. Watson)

We hear of student radicals, political radicals, and terrorists, but where today are the radicals for Jesus? If anybody is radical, it should be us! Our Lord was the most radical person that ever lived. He spoke the most radical words, did the most radical things, and, to cap it all, he rose from the dead. His disciples too were radicals who turned the world upside down with their message. Ten of the original twelve were martyred for their faith, while Peter and John rejoiced that they were counted worthy to suffer shame for the Lord (Acts 5:41). Church history is also filled with radicals for Christ; Polycarp singing praises to God and praying for his captors as he burned to death at the stake; Thomas Cranmer putting his hand, which had written a renunciation of Christ, into a fire, and later being burned at the stake; Martin Luther, proclaiming at the Diet of Worms, his life threatened, "Here I stand, I can do no other – so help me God." The Reformers, Moravians, Methodists, Anabaptists, Salvation Army, and the Student Volunteer Movement, were all radicals who "did not love their lives so much as to shrink from death" (Rev. 12:11).

Many of these other causes require, and receive, total commitment from their members in the spreading of their particular gospel. The Mormons, for example, require all their young men to spend two years on the mission field spreading their doctrine from door to door. Other people give their time and energy to protests against nuclear arms, wars, unfair wages, and a hundred other such causes. How much more, then, should we who have received eternal life lay down our lives to see every kindred tongue, people, and nation share the same eternal life? How much more should we, by the power of the Spirit, be overcoming personal sin and faults so that we might walk in purity and holiness and truly shine as lights in the world? How much more should we be ready to give up the luxuries, and even some of the legitimate pleasures, of this life to bring joy to our heavenly Father's heart, and bring eternal life, and light, to those who sit in darkness?

John R. Mott, the outstanding Christian leader responsible, in large part, for the founding of the Student Volunteer Movement at the turn of the century, had this challenge for his, and future, generations:

I must work the works of Him that sent me while it is day; the night cometh when no man can work. Therefore friends, in view of the awful need of men who are living tonight without Christ; in view of the infinite possibilities of the life related to Christ as mighty Saviour and risen Lord; in view of the impending crisis and urgency of the situation; in view of the conditions which favour a great onward movement within the Church of God; in view of the dangers of anything less than a great onward movement; in view of the great cloud of witnesses who gather around us, of those who subdued kingdoms and wrought righteousness – yes, in view of the constraining memories of the cross of

Christ and the love wherewith He has loved us, let us
rise and resolve, at whatever cost of self-denial, that
live or die, we shall live or die for the evangelisation of
the world in our day. (Quoted in Ralph Winter (ed.),
Perspectives on the World Christian Movement, p. 271.)

EVANGELICAL OR EVANGELISTIC

In the last few years some good books have been published discussing evangelicalism, and all arrive at the
same conclusion – not all evangelicals are evangelistic!
Many, it seems, are evangelical in their beliefs – the deity
of Christ, the Virgin Birth, the death and resurrection
of Jesus, and the like, but few are actively seeking to
propagate their faith. Why is this? After all, we have the
words of eternal life to give a lost and dying world. We
hold the keys to an eternity in heaven or hell. We know
our obedience in spreading the faith brings great joy to
the heart of God. Yet, for one reason or another we
neglect to share with others, and fall into the grip of
either apathy or guilt for failing to do so. I believe,
however, that most Christians want to be effective in
evangelism. They are not satisfied with being a secret
agent Christian or a "silent witness". They know what
the Bible says our obligations are in respect to evangelism
and they want to obey – they simply lack understanding
of how to obey.

One day, on the shore of lake Gennesaret, Jesus helped
Peter to better understand the nature of evangelism, and
the call he had placed on his life, by using the imagery of
fishing. After helping him catch a large amount of fish,
Jesus turned to Peter and said, "Don't be afraid; from
now on you will catch men" (Luke 5:10). Being a fisherman, Peter knew exactly what Jesus had meant, since the

word he used literally means, "to catch men alive". Jesus wants us to go fishing, spiritually speaking, catch men and bring them back alive!

A great many Christians really want to be fishers of men but are frustrated by the huge gap between hearing what they should be doing and actually getting out and doing it. I stumbled upon this "Parable on Fishing" by John Drescher recently and it describes well this dilemma we feel:

"Now it came to pass that a group existed who called themselves fishermen. And lo, there were many fish in the waters all around. And the fish were hungry.

"Week after week, month after month, and year after year, these, who called themselves fishermen, met in meetings and talked about their call to fish, the abundance of fish, and how they might go about fishing.

"These fishermen built large, beautiful buildings called 'Fishing Headquarters'. The plea was that everyone should be a fisherman and every fisherman should fish. One thing they didn't do, however, they didn't fish.

"Finally, after one stirring meeting on 'The Necessity for Fishing', one young fellow left the meeting and went fishing. The next day he reported he had caught two outstanding fish. He was honoured for his excellent catch and scheduled to visit all the big meetings possible to tell how he did it. So he quit his fishing in order to have time to tell other fishermen about the experience. He was also placed on the Fishermen's General Board as a person having considerable experience.

"Now it's true that many of the fishermen sacrificed and put up with all kinds of difficulties. Some lived near the water and bore the smell of dead fish every day. They received the ridicule of some who made fun of their fishermen's clubs and the fact that they claimed to be fishermen yet never fished. They wondered about those who felt it was of little use to attend the weekly meetings to talk about fishing. After all, were they not following the Master who said, 'Follow me, and I will make you fishers of men?' "

No matter how much we talk about evangelism and our desire to bring lost men and women to faith in Christ, talk will not get the job done. The job will only be done when each of us goes, in obedience to Christ, and makes disciples of all nations. Are you seeing your friends, family, and neighbours evangelised? Are you witnessing to them and leading them to faith in Christ? That is what this book is all about – crossing that gulf between hearing what we should be doing in evangelism and actually doing it. It is a practical book that will teach you how you can reach out to people around you, from the unreached tribes of Irian Jaya to your next door neighbour, with a gospel that is "the power of God for the salvation of everyone who believes" (Rom. 1:16).

I believe in the body of Christ today there is a sleeping giant. This giant is made up of the vast majority of Christians who work in the nine-to-five working world, and who feel they do not have time to be involved in evangelism. I was talking recently with a discouraged-looking brother who said to me, "Danny, the western way of life doesn't fit too well with the Great Commission." At first I agreed with him, but as I thought about it later I began to see one of Satan's greatest lies – Christians do not think they can be effective for God in evangelism unless they are in a *full-time* ministry, or are somehow, mysteriously, endowed with great evangelistic gifts that enable them to leap tall buildings in a single bound! The fact of the matter is, however, that we will be effective for God, if we start to witness right where we are, in our job, at home, in our sports club, or wherever. God wants us to be faithful in the little before he makes us ruler over much (Luke 16:10).

Often we shy away from evangelism altogether because we have a preconceived idea, which is more often cultural than biblical, of what it takes to be effective. We think we do not really have what it takes and "compare ourselves with ourselves" (2 Cor. 10:12) and all too often come up on the short end of the stick! When we're not as eloquent as Billy Graham, as bold as Arthur Blessitt, or as flamboyant as Mario Murillo, we seek refuge behind the protective walls of our Christian community and have little contact with the world. We need to start realising, however, that each of us is unique and special to the Lord of the Harvest who desires to use us in his own particular way. One of Satan's greatest tricks is to keep us blinded to this – after all, if the prince of darkness can get us to accept "superstar" theology – that evangelism is the job of the select few – then he has won a major victory over us. We need to see that we are called of God, and our spiritual gifts and personalities are God-given factors which he, as the Master Potter, wants to take, shape and mould so that we become his witnesses – ambassadors to a lost and dying world.

A LIFESTYLE OF EVANGELISM

To the Jews I became like a Jew, to win the Jews; to those under the law, I became like one under the law (though I myself am not under the law) so as to win those under the law; to those not having the law, I became like one not having the law (though I am not free from God's law but am under Christ's law) so as to win those not having the law. To the weak I became weak, to win the weak; I have become all things to all men, so that by all possible means I might save some. I do all this for the sake of the gospel, that I may share in its blessings (1 Cor. 9:20–3).

If evangelism can once again become the lifestyle for the layman of our churches, and reach right to the grass roots of church life, then finishing the task would be within our reach. Michael Green has written concerning early church evangelism:

Communicating the faith was not regarded as the preserve of the very zealous or of the officially designated evangelist. Evangelism was the duty of every church member. The ordinary people of the church saw it as their job: Christianity was supremely a lay movement, spread by informal missionaries. Men will not believe that Christians have good news to share until they find that bishops and bakers, university professors and housewives, bus drivers and street corner preachers are all alike keen to pass it on, however different their methods may be. (Michael Green, *Evangelism in the Early Church*, p. 274.)

A few years ago, I was having a discussion about the need for having a lifestyle of evangelism with a prospective missionary on a church-planting team. He told me that he was doing little or no outreach on his job, but that when he got to the mission field he would begin winning and discipling people. As he told me of his plans, I warned him that if he was not witnessing on his job then he was going to find it difficult to witness on the mission field. He was under the false impression that somehow, magically, automatically, he was going to become a missionary as soon as he reached the mission field. However, it has been said, a missionary is not one who crosses the sea, but one who sees the Cross! If you have seen the Cross, but struggle with crossing the sea, or even the street, to tell someone about Jesus, then I pray that the following tips will help you.

CONDITIONS FOR A LIFESTYLE OF EVANGELISM

1. Get right with God – a pure heart

There is a tendency for people in the church to want the power of God without first having the purity of God.

King David fell into this trap, and could not properly or effectively represent God's salvation until he confessed his sin, repented, and asked God for a new start. "Create in me a pure heart, O God, and renew a steadfast spirit within me. Do not cast me from your presence or take your Holy Spirit from me. Restore to me the joy of your salvation; and grant me a willing spirit, to sustain me. *Then I will teach transgressors your ways; and sinners will turn back to you*" (Psalm 51:10–13).

God desires to develop Christ-like character *in us* before he gives us Christ-honouring fruit in our evangelism. We are told by Peter to add goodness to our faith, then knowledge, self-control, perseverance, godliness, brotherly kindness, and love (2 Peter 1:5–6). He says, "for if you possess these qualities in increasing measure they will keep you from being ineffective and unproductive in your knowledge of our Lord Jesus Christ" (2 Peter 1:8). In the end, we will only be effective in evangelism if the power of God is working through us. He promises to "strengthen those whose hearts are fully committed to him" (2 Chron. 16:9). That is the promise, but the condition is that we diligently make sure our heart is completely his, free of sin, and unspotted from the world (James 1:27). God wants clean vessels doing his work, and the cleaner you are from sin and self the more he can use you.

2. Be filled with the Spirit

"You will receive power when the Holy Spirit comes on you, and you will be my witnesses in Jerusalem, and in all Judea and Samaria, and to the ends of the earth" (Acts 1:8). Note that the power here was given for the express purpose that they might become witnesses.

In 1871 D. L. Moody, one of America's greatest evangelists, was preaching at a service in Chicago. As he preached he noticed two of the ladies on the front pew were busy in fervent prayer, and they later informed him they were praying that he would receive the power of the Holy Spirit. It was not long after this that Moody felt a hunger for a deeper experience with the power of God come over his soul. He describes the experience this way:

> I was crying all the time that God would fill me with His Spirit. Well, one day, in the city of New York – oh, what a day – I cannot describe it; it is almost too sacred an experience to name. I can only say God revealed himself to me, and I had such an experience of His love that I had to ask Him to stay His hand. I went to preaching again. The sermons were not different, yet hundreds were converted. I would not now be placed back where I was before that blessed experience if you should give me all the world – it would be as the small dust of the balance. (J. Gilchrist Lawson, *Deeper Experiences of Famous Christians*, p. 247.)

Paul declared to the Corinthians, regarding the gospel message he had preached to them, "My message and my preaching were not with wise and persuasive words, but with a demonstration of the Spirit's power" (1 Cor. 2:4). He understood how pointless it would be to try to win people from spiritual darkness to light using only carnal means. We need to allow the Holy Spirit to fill us to overflowing so that our evangelism will become as effective as it can posibly be. There are no two ways about it, if you want to be effective in evangelism, then you must be filled with God's Holy Spirit. You may be Baptist and believe you get the power at conversion. You may be Pentecostal and believe you need to speak in tongues to prove you have got it. You may be Charismatic and believe you must have hands laid on you to get it. You may believe you need to tarry in Jerusalem, visit Azusa Street, or whatever, but as Catherine Booth once said, "It doesn't matter how you get it, just get it!" The world that Jesus died for is at stake, so we must do God's work in his way, and that way is always, Spirit-filled and Spirit-led.

3. Get your priorities right

Do your priorities line up with God's priorities? When people tell me they are not being effective in evangelism I usually ask how important winning the lost is to them. Is it a priority, does it play a big part in your day-to-day living? You can easily tell what your highest priorities really are by simply gauging how much time you spend doing various activities. How much time do you spend praying about the effectiveness of your evangelism? How often do you pray for the lost? When is the last time you prayed and fasted for someone's salvation? Do you pray for missionaries and wage spiritual warfare against the forces of darkness over the world? Do you give money to gospel work and missions, and are you willing to give God more than one seventh of your week and one tenth of your money? Allow the Holy Spirit to search your heart as you answer these questions and seek to determine the right priority for evangelism in your life. A lost and dying world was so high on God's priority list that "he gave his one and only Son, that whoever believes in him should not perish but have eternal life" (John 3:16). How high is that lost world on your priority list?

4. Be available

An old preacher once said, "God is not looking for ability, but availability." When Isaiah saw the Lord's glory he also painfully saw his own inabilities and cried out, "I am ruined! For I am a man of unclean lips, and I live among a people of unclean lips" (Isa. 6:5). God, however, did not condemn him for his shortcomings, but purged his sin and asked who was available. "Whom shall I send, and who will go for us?" Isaiah's enthusiastic response was, "Here am I; send me" (Isa. 6:8). All too often our response goes something like this, "Here I am: SEND HIM!"

as we point to someone we feel is more suited for the task
than us. But there is no one else. No one else can do
exactly what you can do in the sphere of influence you are
in. God needs ambassadors for his kingdom in every area
of life. Our response needs to be, "Lord, I'm available,
maybe I'm not much, but I'll give you all of me there is to
use in reaching a lost world. Lord, help me to bring them
back alive."

I remember an old film from the 1930s called *The Green
Pastures*, which portrayed how black children in the
south pictured God and heaven. In the film there was a
scene where God asked Abraham, Isaac and Jacob for
their counsel on who would be a good candidate to
deliver his children from bondage in Egypt. The trio
talked it over and asked the Lord, "Do you want the
brainiest, or the holiest?" The Lord quickly responded, "I
want the holiest, I can make him brainy!" Although the
film had some obvious theological problems, it still portrayed an important truth. As long as we are there to offer
ourselves "as living sacrifices, holy and pleasing to God"
(Rom. 12:1), he can make us "brainy" or mould us into
whatever he chooses. He chooses the foolish things, the
base things, to do his work. God's army is not an army of
conscripts, it is made up of soldiers of the cross who are
willing and available.

5. Expect God to use you

"Without faith it is impossible to please God" (Heb. 11:6).
Someone has said, about shooting an arrow, "If you aim
at nothing, then you'd better be careful, you might hit it!"
Sometimes we do not expect God to use us and end up
getting just what we expected – nothing! We need to
believe that he will use us. The Bible promises that if we
dwell in Christ we will be fruitful, "If a man remains in
me and I in him, he will bear much fruit" (John 15:5). If
we abide in Christ we should be expecting to bear fruit.

William Carey, pioneer missionary to India, said, "Expect great things from God, attempt great things for God." According to Jesus the field is ready for harvest, and all that is needed is for people to believe he has spoken the truth and go and gather in the harvest. You may say, "But how could God use me?" That attitude is exactly what qualifies you for his grace; the more you realise you cannot do it, and the less confidence you have in yourself, the more you can trust him to do it through you. "Commit your way to the Lord; trust in him, and he will do this" (Psalm 37:5).

6. Ask the Lord for opportunities to share your faith

A friend of mine used to end his letters with the phrase. "Don't keep the faith – spread it." No matter where you are, you can think of unbelievers, names and faces who you have regular contact with, be they relatives, fellow workers, friends, garage attendants, or even an ice cream seller in the park, who are all people that Jesus died for, and who could be reached through you. Perhaps you are the only Christian contact they will ever have. God challenges us, "Ask of me, and I will make the nations your inheritance, the ends of the earth your possession" (Psalm 2:8). We need to accept this challenge, ask God for specific opportunities to share our faith with those mentioned above, and then wait expectantly. Often the door is already open but we have missed it by not expecting it to be. We should be like the horse at the starting gate, he is waiting, but waiting *aggressively*, for the gate to open so that he can throw himself into the race. God wants you to witness for him, all we have to do is be ready and waiting, then he can use us to "do immeasurably more than all we ask or imagine, according to his power that is at work within us" (Eph. 3:20).

7. Practise personal evangelism

I know the word "practise" often sounds like a dirty
word to many Christians, but even Billy Graham did not
start out by preaching to thousands: instead he practised
his God-given gift on much smaller groups. We need to
develop a lifestyle of evangelism, but like most things in
life it takes practice. Personal evangelism is you, with all
your strengths, weaknesses, idiosyncrasies, fears, and
gifts, sharing with someone else that they can have a
relationship with the most important person in the universe – Jesus Christ. Paul told Timothy to fan the flame of
his spiritual gift (2 Tim. 1:6) and do the work of an
evangelist (2 Tim. 4:5). You may not be an evangelist –
neither was Timothy – but we are all called to be
witnesses, and this requires the exercising of our
evangelistic muscles.

I love surfing. If someone comes and asks me to teach
them to surf the best thing I can tell them to do is, get on a
board and try it. I could give them Nat Young's book on
the history of surfing, or a book on oceanography, even a
subscription to *Surfer* magazine, but none of these things
would help unless they go out and try it. In the same way
that you learn to surf by spending time on a board in the
water, you also learn to witness by witnessing. You can
study the various witnessing techniques – Four Spiritual
Laws, Four Facts of Life, Five Steps To Peace With God,
Six Quantum Leaps to Christ! – whatever – and they are
all good. However, they may not necessarily be you!
When evangelism is worked into a lifestyle then it becomes the natural outflow of what is inside you. It is
spontaneous and alive, and not just a pat formula. It is
"Christ in you, the hope of glory" (Col. 1:27). We need to
practise opening the "glory spout" and let the glory out,
and I cannot tell you exactly how to do that, because I am
not you. I can give you some principles in the following
chapters that, with the Lord's help, will teach you how to
touch a lost and dying land with the living water that

flows out of you, but only you can decide to open up and let that water come bubbling out. When all the principles of effective evangelism have been written, the decision to take them up and use them lies with you. Are you going to be effective in evangelism? You can be, the choice is yours!

Chapter 2

Paul's principles of evangelism:

Lessons from Thessalonica – I

In the opening verses of Acts 17 we find the Apostle Paul in the Macedonian city of Thessalonica, establishing a new church. As a result of his efforts, a thriving base for the evangelisation of Macedonia is founded, to which the letters of First and Second Thessalonians would later be addressed. Paul opens his first letter by commending the Thessalonian believers for their great evangelistic zeal, faith, hope and love in Christ. He goes on to say that because their evangelising has been so effective throughout the entire region on a later visit his team "do not need to say anything" (1 Thess. 1:8).

Paul's success in church-planting at Thessalonica highlights for us some important principles. If we put Acts 17 alongside the Thessalonian Epistles we find it only took Paul three weeks to plant this church successfully ('Acts 17:2). The principles gleaned here, under the guidance of the Holy Spirit, can be used in other situations to promote effective evangelism with long-lasting results. We must be careful, though, not merely to copy Paul's example without first having the Spirit's leading. He is the one to show us how to apply these principles in our own particular situations. "Unless the Lord builds the house its builders labour in vain" (Ps. 127:1).

IDENTIFICATION

Identification in communication

Paul made it a point to identify with the people he was trying to reach (Acts 17:1). He allowed his unbelieving audience to shape what he would say, and how he would say it. Acts 17 records Paul ministering in four different locations – Thessalonica, Berea, Athens and on Athens' Mars Hill. In the first three instances he preached in synagogues, where he would open Isaiah and the Psalms and show that Jesus was the fulfilment of all foretold in the Jewish scriptures. He did not preach from the Jewish scriptures, though, to the philosophers of Mars Hill as they were unauthoritative to pagan philosophers. Instead, he pointed to the altar of the unknown god, a common interest through which he could share the *same* truth as he had in the synagogue. He achieved this by finding a point of interest and identity with the various groups, from which he could communicate with them. Paul realised that in the Thessalonican synagogue preaching from Isaiah 53 and Psalm 22 presented the truth in a way the Jews could relate to, while speaking of the creator God, and quoting from some of their own Greek poets was the way he could identify with the philosophers on Mars Hill, and help them better to understand what he was saying.

Identification in living

Jesus is our supreme example of identification. He became one of us in order that he might reach us. Likewise, Paul explained that he had "become all things to all men, so that by all possible means I might save some" (1 Cor. 9:22). It is not always easy to find the correct balance between identification with, and separation from, the world. Just how far we should go is between each individual and the Lord, and we need continually to look to him for that balance. There are instances in history, however, when it was necessary to step outside cultural norms.

Hudson Taylor, a young man with a burden for China, took the bold step of leaving England to live among the Chinese. However, he found he was, in large part, ineffective in sharing with the Chinese. Pondering on the problem, he realised the need for greater identification, and so began to eat Chinese food, learned the Chinese language, and grew his hair until it was long enough to braid like the Chinese he wanted to reach. Though frowned upon by many of his contemporary missionaries, and widely misunderstood at home, Taylor's results were astounding. Eventually he founded one of the most successful cross-cultural missionary movements in the history of the church, the China Inland Mission Society, which today, as the Overseas Missionary Fellowship, still thrives.

In 1962, Don and Carol Richardson moved to Irian Jaya as missionaries to the cannibalistic, stone-age, Sawi people. Here, they found a people among whom treachery was considered the highest virtue, and who were hardened to the gospel. When Don and Carol tried to explain the death and resurrection of Christ to the Sawi, Judas became the hero of the story for them, and his kiss of betrayal delighted them as the ultimate act of virtue. As the Richardsons sought God for an answer to their dilemma they discovered a cultural key that would unlock the true meaning of the gospel to the Sawi. They observed that when the Sawis made peace with another tribe they would exchange babies as a covenant of peace between them. If war was declared on each other again then each tribe would kill the other's "peace child". Don and Carol explained to the Sawi that Jesus was God's peace child whom he had sent to bring reconciliation between himself and the world. This new perspective on the gospel resulted in hundreds of the tribe accepting the peace of Christ as they were reconciled to God. These two sensitive missionaries were able to see a major break-through of the gospel among the Sawi because they had identified with them and their culture.

In the late 1960s and early 1970s Chuck Smith, a pastor from a small church in southern California called Calvary Chapel, began to feel God's heart for the hippies who were turning to drugs and the occult, and away from the church. As he prayed about how to reach hippies, God directed Lonnie Frisbee to him. Lonnie was a young long-haired evangelist with a passion for winning hippies to the Lord. As a result, God's power was tremendously demonstrated in both conversions and healings, and today there are many Calvary Chapels across America, some of which have grown to have thousands in their membership. It all started when God found someone who was willing to identify with the people he wanted to reach.

"Jesus music" was a tool greatly used by God during this period. Innovators such as Larry Norman, Chuck Girard and Paul Clark combined contemporary music styles with Christian lyrics in order to reach the young. In so doing they pioneered the way for hundreds of others to use music as a point of identification with lost youth.

HERITAGE FACTOR

Paul took advantage of this "heritage factor" in his evangelism (Acts 17:2). A study of his missionary journeys shows a definite and carefully planned strategy in the visits he made to various cities of the ancient world. He would go to a city, find the local synagogue, and seek to preach the gospel there; we are told this was "his custom". The synagogues contained three groups of

people; Jews (natural children of Israel); Jewish proselytes (Gentiles who had joined themselves by circum-
cision); and God-fearers (Gentiles who believed in and
feared God, but who stopped short of becoming
proselytes).

Often rejected and persecuted by the Jewish sector,
Paul would form the nucleus of his new church from the
God-fearing Gentiles, who already believed in the God of
the Old Testament and needed only to be instructed in
the gospel message. They were "ripe", and Paul took
advantage of their scriptural heritage, to reap a rich
harvest of souls in the places he visited. Comparing the
results in Thessalonica, where there was a heritage factor, and where "many of the Jews believed, as did also a
number of prominent Greek women and many Greek
men" (Acts 17:12) and Mars Hill where there was no
heritage factor and only "a few men . . . believed" (Acts
17:34), is very enlightening. Paul went to the religious
people first, in much the same way Jesus primarily went
to the Jews (Matt. 15:24). The gospel was to go to Jews
first (Rom. 1:16), the Gentiles would be grafted in at a
later date (Rom. 11).

In many nations today where significant church
growth is taking place we often find much of the ground
work has been done by earlier Christian workers who
have given the people a heritage factor, rendering them
receptive to the gospel. In Latin America, for example, it
was the Catholic missionaries who laid the ground work
that has resulted in the rapid growth of the church in
Brazil, Guatemala, Argentina and other countries of the
region. The same is true of the Protestant missionaries
who pioneered the way for the staggering growth of the
church in South Korea, Indonesia, South Africa and even
North America. When Jesus spoke of the harvest field, he
spoke of reaping the benefit of another man's labours
(John 4:38). Paul understood what this meant and, as it
were, harvested where the Jews had already planted the
seed.

In America 75 per cent of the population claims to believe in God and most give mental assent, at least, to the notion that Jesus was more than a man. So, having a heritage factor, we must go out and build on it, and see many won to the Lord. In surveys of average evangelical churches and training schools, I found that over 50 per cent of those surveyed came from some type of "Christian" upbringing, be it nominally Catholic or Protestant.

I met John Pipolo one day while street witnessing, and my wife and I soon became good friends with him and his brother Anthony. They were in a sense true twentieth-century "God-fearers" from a strong Italian Catholic background. We began visiting them from time to time to share the gospel, but eventually we lost contact with each other. Other Christians though, shared the love of Jesus with them, through both personal testimony and litera-ture. John and Anthony were encouraged to follow Jesus, and eventually did, along with John's wife, mother, sister and older brother. Today the Pipolo family are among some of the most committed Christians I know. Their strong Catholic heritage provided a wonder-ful foundation on which to build.

A common mistake is to disregard the heritage factor. Often, in our desire to put people right about their beliefs we end up alienating them. When we attack Roman Catholics over their belief in the mass, rosary, and the Virgin Mary, we destroy the foundation God has given us to build on in their life, so alienating them from us. We cannot allow ourselves to be sidetracked from the central issue – their relationship with Jesus Christ.

In discussing the heritage factor I am not suggesting that we only attempt to reach those with "suitable" backgrounds. There are millions of people not receptive to the gospel, who have no heritage factor, and we need workers to go and prepare the way for them to receive the message of salvation. If, however, we are in an area that has a Christian heritage it will be to our distinct advantage to build upon it as we share the gospel.

CONSISTENCY

Paul was consistent in his evangelism, ". . . as his custom was . . ." (Acts 17:2). He understood the principle that if you sow sparingly, you will also reap sparingly (2 Cor. 9:6) and his evangelism reflected this. A farmer does not merely sow a few seeds here and there and expect to gather in a great harvest from it. Instead, he carefully prepares the ground and plants a lot of seed. Likewise, no commercial fisherman will fish only when he feels like it, but will continually let down his nets, repositioning his boat until he has an adequate catch. From this we can learn an important lesson.

Evangelist Arthur Blessitt tells of a young man who came to him complaining about his unfruitfulness in evangelism, and wondering why Arthur was so effective in his endeavours. Arthur asked him how often he witnessed to unbelievers. "Every once in a while, as the spirit leads," was the young man's reply. "That's the difference between you and me," Arthur responded, "I witness to almost everyone, everywhere I go, and I can't imagine anyone that the Lord wouldn't want me to witness to." The fruit of his ministry speaks to the validity of this philosophy. Arthur Blessitt believes in being consistent.

Not only must we be consistent in planting the seed of the gospel in people's hearts, but also in watering that seed. Often we give up on a person we have witnessed to because there was no immediate response. What is really needed is to build a relationship with the person and, over time, we are more likely to see them come to the Lord. Surveys suggest that as many as 80 per cent of all converts to Christianity are the direct result of personal witness from a Christian friend.

APOLOGETICS

The Greek word "apologia", used several times in the New Testament, means to make a rational defence of the gospel. Paul did exactly that in his evangelism, ". . . on three sabbath days he *reasoned* with them from the Scriptures, explaining and proving" (Acts 17:2–3). The Philippians were told that Paul was, "put here for the defence (*apologia*) of the gospel" (Phil. 1:17). Likewise, Peter tells us to give an ". . . answer to everyone who asks you to give the reason for the hope that you have" (1 Peter 3:15).

Using apologetics in evangelism, or reasoning with someone about their faith, does not necessarily reveal a lack of trust in the power of God. Often it helps a person's understanding as spiritual blinkers are removed (2 Cor. 4:4). Some say we should never defend the truth, for truth defends itself. If only that were true – but it is not. We are exhorted by Jude to "contend for the faith that was once for all entrusted to the saints" (Jude 3). If we can keep our cool and, in reasonably disagreeing with someone, show them the truth, then we should take advantage of the opportunity.

While at my friend Alex's home one night, two Jehovah's Witnesses knocked at the door. Inviting them in we began to discuss the Bible, and slowly our discussion turned into the typical Bible argument between a Christian and a Jehovah's Witness. It was not heated, but there were definite disagreements regarding Jehovah's Witness' theology and the integrity of the "Watchtower" as God's prophet. After four and a half hours of reasoning with them one, Janet, was convinced of her error and gave her life over to Jesus. She has been serving the Lord ever since. Discussions often generate a lot of heat and little light but, with the Spirit's guidance, we can provide people with reasons for faith in an atmosphere of love and trust, and see them come to understand and know Jesus.

The most valuable apologetic tool is the Bible itself. Ample evidence for its claim to be God's Word has come from fulfilled prophecy, archaeological findings, and the examination of over 24,000 manuscripts that attest to its truthfulness. Such facts can be helpful in enlightening a mind bound by spiritual darkness. *Presuppositional* apologetics is also a helpful tool in this regard. With it we attempt to discover what a person believes and why they believe it. We then draw their belief system to its logical conclusions, showing the fallacy of such a system. This is often enlightening for a non-believer since many have never thought through what they believe very thoroughly. We can also contrast their belief system with one based on Biblical truth.

Keep in mind that apologetics alone will not draw a person into the Kingdom of God. Faith comes by hearing the Word of God (Rom. 10:17). Apologetics' value, however, lies in the fact that, with the application of truth, we can strip away blinkers from unbelieving minds held captive by Satan (2 Cor. 4:4), opening the way for the light of the gospel to come in. I have witnessed and reasoned with some people who have come to see the truth of the gospel very clearly, but have still failed to respond to it. We must not forget that it is the Holy Spirit alone, and not reason, that ultimately convicts a person of their sin (John 16:8).

Many books have been published on apologetics, and they are a valuable resource when seeking to communicate the gospel to a mind blinded by philosophy, Ideology, tradition, a religious cult, or sin. Authors such as Josh McDowell, C. S. Lewis, Francis Shaeffer, John Warwick Montgomery and Walter Martin, have all written on the subject and the knowledge they have to share would benefit us all. Francis Shaeffer said, "We must be prepared to give honest answers to the honest questions of our generation." Apologetics allows us to do just that. "Always be prepared to give an *answer* to every one" (1 Pet. 3:15).

SIMPLICITY – THE BIBLICAL GOSPEL

Paul preached the simple gospel, "explaining and proving that the Christ had to suffer and rise from the dead". "This Jesus I am proclaiming to you is the Christ," he said (Acts 17:3).

Despite his education Paul did not use "eloquence or superior wisdom", and determined to know nothing among the Corinthians "except Jesus Christ and him crucified" (1 Cor. 2:2). Later he warned the same church that Satan would try to lead them away from the simplicity that is in Christ (2 Cor. 11:3).

With all our modern techniques of evangelism and apologetics we must never forget that the preaching of the Cross is the "power of God for the salvation of everyone who believes" (Rom. 1:16). The power of the gospel message can, and has, brought millions to the foot of the Cross for forgiveness. So, the focal point of our message, no matter how we proclaim it, must be that Jesus died on the Cross for our sin and rose again from the dead (1 Cor. 15:3–4).

It is said that becoming a Christian is a subjective experience based upon objective truth, and we must be careful to present the Jesus of history as well as the Jesus of our experience. Christianity is true, but not just because you have personally experienced it. *It is truth whether you have experienced it or not!* If we preach solely from experience, without reference to the historical facts of Jesus' death and resurrection, we are only preaching half the truth. What happens if you backslide? Does that render the gospel untrue? No, regardless of whether men respond to Jesus or not, it does not change the fact that he really did die, and really did rise again from the dead!

Before I was a Christian I used to take drugs with my cousin Lee. After my conversion I went back to see him and tell him of my experience with Jesus. I explained that I did not need drugs any more because Jesus had given me the peace and joy I longed for – he was my new "high". Lee responded enthusiastically, and told me how he had been "saved" from the drug lifestyle as well! However, his salvation had not come from Jesus, but through the Maharishi's transcendental meditation. As he described his new-found joy and peace it became a battle of testimonies – my peace is better than your peace!!

From that encounter I learned two important things. Firstly, we must not communicate the gospel as though Jesus is just another experience that will get you higher than hash! Secondly, our testimony is not enough on its own. We need to share the biblical gospel and lift up the Jesus of history, as well as the Jesus of our personal experience. Our testimonies are valid, even a weapon in spiritual warfare (Rev. 12:11) and should be used as the Lord leads. But we must be careful to do as Paul did, and preach Jesus – crucified, buried and risen again.

Evangelism is proclamation of the good news to the lost, and cannot be defined in terms of results since we know, from both scripture and experience, that not all who hear are going to be saved. There is a difference between witnessing, *proclaiming* the good news; and con-verting *persuading* a person to receive Christ. Because Jesus is our Lord and has commanded us to preach the gospel to every creature, we do, regardless of results. However, Jesus also promises that if we abide in him we will bear fruit. In the end, however, fruit is not the issue, as much as obedience to the Lord in the proclamation of the gospel. We can be sure we have evangelised someone if we have faithfully proclaimed the gospel message to them. The results then are up to him.

PREACHING AMIDST OPPOSITION

Paul preached despite opposition, "the Jews were jealous; so they rounded up some bad characters from the market place, formed a mob and started a riot in the city" (Acts 17:5).

Wherever Paul went there was either a revival or a riot, but he did not let this slow him down, since he knew from the start that his call to preach would result in persecution (Acts 9:16). He was aware that chains and affliction awaited him in every city yet his response was, "However, I consider my life worth nothing to me, if only I may finish the race and complete the task the Lord has given me – the task of testifying to the gospel of God's grace" (Acts 20:24). The New Testament constantly reminds us that believers are called to suffer for the gospel's sake (Matt. 5:11; 10:22; 13:21; Rom. 8:17, 36; 2 Cor. 1:7; Phil. 1:29; 2 Tim. 2:12; 1 Peter 5:10).

Persecution and opposition should not be regarded as uncommon intruders into our work – hard situations provide God with opportunities to show his greatness on our behalf. He may choose to deliver us from the trial, or deliver us in the trial. Our responsibility is to be faithful to him as he works "all things together for good" (Rom. 8:28).

"If we endure, we will also reign with him . . ." (2 Tim. 2:12). Never go looking for persecution, but, if it comes, do not stop doing his work. It is easy to be tempted to give up evangelism when we encounter opposition to our work. We need to bear in mind, though, that there is a war for the souls of men going on around us, and Satan would love to see us discouraged and defeated.

"Everyone who wants to live a godly life in Christ Jesus will be persecuted" (2 Tim. 3:12). When we live as God wants us to, the devil will get angry! Once we determine to live or die for the evangelisation of the world, we will draw Satan's attacks, as honey attracts bees. Satan is after those who pose a threat to his kingdom, but Jesus is the victor. Hallelujah!

Scripture tells us to stand against the schemes of the devil (Eph. 6:11). Satan is crafty in his attacks on God's children, using any, and every, means to stop our effectiveness. Sometimes he comes like a lion – perhaps a Muslim fanatic trying to kill us. At other times he will appear as an angel of light (2 Cor. 11:14), bringing a false doctrine that tickles our ears and appeals to the flesh. Other times he uses well-meaning Christians who exhort us to experience the "good life" of health and wealth, while we miss God's call for our life. Do not be ignorant of Satan's devices (2 Cor. 2:11). Opposition in evangelism comes simply because we are seeking to set spiritual prisoners free (2 Tim. 2:26) and Satan will not let them go easily!

As well as Satan's opposition, we will also experience human opposition! People do not like to be told they need to change – selfish people do not enjoy being challenged to deny themselves. There is a built-in offence in the gospel message (Gal. 5:11) and when it is preached with power it stirs reactions that range from total acceptance to apathy, indifference and outright persecution. We must be prepared for this, and not allow any type of persecution to deter us. Solomon warns, "The sluggard will not plough by reason of the cold: therefore shall he beg in harvest, and have nothing" (Prov. 20:4 AV). We cannot allow opposition to hinder our work in God's harvest field. Instead we must determine in our hearts to be committed in doing Christ's will and bringing pleasure to his heart.

> And though the earth with devils filled
> Will threaten to undo us,

We will not fear for God hath willed
His truth to triumph through us.
Let goods and kindred go,
This mortal life also.
The body they may kill;
God's truth abideth still
And we must win the battle.

(Martin Luther)

KINGDOM PREACHING

Paul preached the kingdom of God: ". . . they dragged Jason and some other brothers before the city officials shouting: 'These men who have caused trouble all over the world have now come here [. . .] saying that there is another king, one called Jesus'" (Acts 17:6–7).

Paul and his team turned the world upside down by preaching that Jesus was King and rightful ruler over all the earth. They did not see Jesus as an optional extra to be added to the pantheon of gods, but proclaimed him as the divine sovereign with the right to rule over people's lives. The early church had a theological basis for the aggressive evangelism with which they turned the world upside down. Their watchword was, "Jesus is Lord". He *is* King and desires to bring his rule and reign to this earth; ". . . your Kingdom come, your will be done on earth as it is in heaven" (Matt. 6:10).

Understanding this will help us to be bold in our evangelism. We are not a people grovelling in the dirt of the devil's world, begging others to accept Jesus as their "personal Saviour". Rather, we are a people who realise, "The earth is the Lord's, and everything in it, the world, and all who live in it" (Psalm 24:1). We have been given a mandate, "The kingdom of God is near. Repent and believe the good news!'' (Mark 1:15) and do not need to be intimidated by people as we witness. We, after all, not only have the responsibility, but the right, to carry out the work of evangelism, because of the authority of him who has commanded us to do so.

The fullness of the kingdom of God will not come until Jesus returns, but the church here and now must seek to establish Christ's reign in every area of life. We must be a prophetic voice against evil and injustice. The plight of the poor, and murder of the unborn, for example, should be of serious concern to us who represent the King. We are to be the salt of the earth, as well as the light of the world (Matt. 5:13–14). The presence of the kingdom of God should be a restraining force (salt) against the evil of this world, while, at the same time being a positive force for good (light).

The educational system needs teachers and students who can uphold righteousness and make a stand against humanism. Countries need politicians who will lead the people of God, implementing his principles of justice and righteousness in secular government. The sports world needs heroes that can point to the King as the source of their strength. The world desperately needs to see Christian marriages and families that represent Christ's love for the church.

The church is the expression of the kingdom of God on earth, and our personal holiness, love for one another, concern over the poor and social issues, commitment to missions, even our physical lifestyle, must all be a reflection of him. When we put his kingdom first, everything else falls into its proper place (Matt. 6:33).

Chapter 3

Paul's principles of evangelism:

Lessons from Thessalonica – II

Shortly after Paul was forced to flee the persecution in Thessalonica he sent Timothy back to see how the infant church was doing. Timothy's report back was full of "good news about their faith and love" (1 Thess. 3:6). Paul then wrote his first epistle to the Thessalonians, from which we can glean further principles Paul used in his evangelism as he pioneered one of the most fruitful of all the early churches.

THE POWER OF GOD

Paul preached in the power of God. "Because our gospel came to you not simply with words, but also with power, with the Holy Spirit and with deep conviction . . ." (1 Thess. 1:5).

Paul understood the message itself was powerful (Rom. 1:16) but that words alone were not sufficient to draw blinded minds and hardened hearts to Jesus, unless God, by his Spirit, first puts his power on those words. He informed the intellectual Greeks of Corinth, "My message and my preaching were not with wise and persuasive words, but with a demonstration of the

Spirit's power, so that your faith might not rest on men's wisdom, but on God's power" (1 Cor. 2:4–5). He resisted the temptation to rely on his own abilities, and relied instead on the power of God to bear witness of the word that was preached with "signs, wonders and various miracles, and gifts of the Holy Spirit" (Heb. 2:4).

God reminds Zerubbabel, "Not by might nor by power, but by my Spirit, says the Lord Almighty." (Zech. 4:6). God designed evangelism in such a way that he will not do it without us, and we cannot do it without him. He is quick to withdraw his hand from our work when we trust in human methods or gimmicks that are devoid of his Spirit, letting us come to the end of our tether so that we will cry out to him for his power and anointing. He wants us to see that there is no substitute in evangelism for his power, and more can be accomplished in a few weeks of ministry in the power of God than can be done through years of powerless preaching.

Shortly after the turn of the century evangelist John G. Lake answered God's call to the mission field of South Africa. After much preaching, without seeing any results, he began to fast and pray. On the twenty-first day of his fast, as he walked down a street in Johannesburg, he noticed a horse had broken its leg, and a policeman's gun was poised ready to put it out of its misery. Lake quickly stretched out his hand and prayed for the horse which was instantly healed, got up, and went on its way. From that point on Lake saw a new church established in South Africa on the average of one every three days! (P. Wagner, *On the Crest of the Wave*, p. 141)

In his book *Thy God Reigneth*, R. Edward Miller relays the story of a powerful visitation of the Holy Spirit in Argentina during 1954. After two and a half years of patient prayer and waiting on God by a group of intercessors, he poured out his Spirit. "Up until that time, the evangelical works were limited. Most of the churches were comparatively small; conversions were here and

there; and healings were few. Who could imagine that
God would move out on a large scale when he had never
done it before!'' Miller goes on to tell how a little-known
American evangelist named Tommy Hicks came to
Argentina, in obedience to the Spirit's leading, to hold an
evangelistic healing campaign. Hicks went to see President Peron and was stopped at the palace door by an
armed guard. He prayed for the guard and saw him
instantly healed, and the next day that guard escorted
him to see the President. Peron suffered from eczema
which no physician seemed able to cure, and which had
progressed to the point where Peron allowed no photographs to be taken of him. Hicks prayed for the President
and he too was instantly healed. This opened the way for
a two-month salvation and healing campaign, which, at
its peak, had over 200,000 people in attendance, with
many being saved and healed of incurable sicknesses
and diseases. The Lord confirmed his word with his
power.

Indonesia, too, has experienced a mighty baptism in
the power of God in recent years. Mel Tari describes the
outpouring in the book *Like A Mighty Wind*. The
preaching of the gospel accompanied by signs and wonders has contributed significantly to the phenomenal
growth of the church in Indonesia since 1966. On the
island of Timor alone the Evangelical Christian Church
grew by 100,000 members in only four years. While other
factors have helped contribute to this influx, Christianity
has gained over two and a half million converts in
Muslim Indonesia since 1965.

Anyone who has been to the mission field and
observed the powers of darkness at work in spiritism,
witchcraft and false religions would agree that for a
significant harvest we will need to see a corresponding
display of the power of God through signs and wonders.
Whenever there is a display of satanic power it needs to
be countered with a greater display of the power of God
(Ex. 7:10–13; Acts 13:6–12; 16:16–18; 1 Jn. 4:4). We see

this demonstrated again and again in the New Testament. The Samaritans "heard Philip and saw the miraculous signs he did" (Acts 8:6). When Peter spoke the word of faith to heal Aeneas, "All who lived in Lydda and Sharon saw him and turned to the Lord" (Acts 9:33–5). As word got around Joppa that Peter had raised Tabitha from the dead, "many people believed in the Lord" (Acts 9:40–2). While Sergius Paulus, the deputy, was saved after seeing Elymas the sorcerer blinded by Paul (Acts 13:11–12). After Jesus healed the nobleman's son the whole family immediately believed in him (Jn 4:47–53).

Perhaps the most effective way to begin moving in this "supernatural evangelism" is to step out and exercise our spiritual gifts among non-Christians. Jesus exercised both the word of wisdom and the word of knowledge when dealing with the woman at the well, (Jn. 4:1–42). He had supernatural wisdom when speaking of living water, and knew the perfect time to speak the word of knowledge he had received from his Father regarding her previous five husbands and present boyfriend. It takes wisdom to win souls (Prov. 11:30) and as we seek God he will at times give to us divine information regarding situations so that we can move effectively in supernatural power.

Recently, several friends and I decided to have an impromptu time of street evangelism. We gathered for our usual pre-outreach prayer time, and some felt impressed by the Lord not to go out witnessing but to stay behind and pray for those who did. I was one of those who went out witnessing, and after an uneventful hour or so approached a young man in the doorway of a bar. After several minutes of conversation with Cliff I found he was not a Christian, but was open and ready to receive. I felt distinctly impressed by the Lord to "press" him for a decision (I'm usually hesitant to do so because I do not want to talk anyone into something someone else can talk them out of!). This time though, I felt I needed not only to *proclaim* but also *persuade*, and, after a couple of hours, Cliff was gloriously saved, and is still walking with the Lord. I did not know at the time, but back at the prayer meeting Christopher, one of the leaders, had received a vision of a young man in a green shirt who was ready to receive and needed to be pressed for a commitment to Christ. In direct response to their intercession I was able to be sensitive to Cliff's need and bring him to Jesus. He was wearing a green shirt too! Again, the next week, we used the same strategy, but this time I was one of those who felt led to stay behind and pray. In the time of intercession God impressed upon me the story of the prodigal son, so we proceeded to pray specifically that God would use our team to bring prodigal sons home. That night two backsliders recommitted their lives to Christ.

Marty, a surfer and lifeguard at a local beach, was a former Christian who had become involved with the occult. A Youth With A Mission outreach team was witnessing on the beach and one of the participants approached Marty with a gospel tract, which was met with cold rejection. The next day, as the outreach team prayed in preparation for their day's witnessing at a local shopping mall, God impressed upon them that they should go back instead to the beach they were at the day before. As they approached the beach God gave several words of knowledge to one of the team members named Dave about Marty's past life. Dave approached Marty and told him facts about his previous conversion, involvement in the occult, and other details of his life, which Dave had no way of knowing. Afterwards Marty was invited to the Youth With A Mission (YWAM) centre to meet me, since we had a similar cultural background. Marty gave his life back to the Lord that night and within a year and a half was working as a medical missionary amongst the poor of the Philippines. However, it took a work of the supernatural to open him up to the truth.

God also demonstrates his power by convicting unbelievers of their sin (Jn. 16:8). Paul told the Thessalonians
that the gospel was preached "With the Holy Spirit and
with deep conviction" (1 Thess. 1:5). Only the Holy Spirit
can convict a person of their sin and show their need of
Jesus for salvation. They must be convicted and convinced they are lost before they will ever want to be
saved. So, we must allow the Spirit to do his convicting
work in a person's heart before we persuade them to
receive Jesus.

Peter's pentecostal sermon illustrates well the work-
ings of the human and divine elements in evangelism.
Peter *proclaimed* the gospel message, and then his
hearers were pierced to the heart and asked Peter and the
apostles what they needed to do (Acts 2:37). After seeing
evidence of the Spirit's convicting work Peter *persuaded*
them to receive Jesus. Proclamation, conviction, and
then persuasion – in that order.

J. Edwin Orr, an authority on evangelical awakenings,
states that one of the common elements in great revivals
of the past is a deep conviction of sin, first in the church,
then in the world. The late Duncan Campbell described
men under conviction during the Hebrides revival crying
out for mercy and saying, "Hell is too good for me, hell is
too good for me." According to accounts of revivalist
preaching of the eighteenth and nineteenth centuries,
people would cry out to God, shrieking and groaning,
sometimes even falling unconscious under the conviction of sin! Before the good news can be received the bad
news must be believed. That is, sinners must know they
are separated from God, and only then, will they seek to
be saved from their sin.

We need the power of God upon us as we evangelise,
and must be prepared to do God's work in God's way,
leaving the results to him. As we carry out the Great
Commission we must seek God continually for his power
to be upon us in anointed preaching, signs and wonders,
conviction of sin, and holy living.

AWARENESS OF HELL

". . . Jesus, who rescues us from the coming wrath" (1 Thess. 1:10). Hell is never pleasant to discuss, but its reality is spelled out again and again as we search the New Testament. Jesus spoke often of an eternal abode of the lost, warning of its danger and describing it as a place of "eternal punishment" (Matt. 25:46) and "the darkness", where there is "weeping and gnashing of teeth" (Matt. 8:12). Peter spoke also of a "blackest darkness' reserved for false teachers (2 Pet. 2:17) and Jude spoke of the "blackest darkness" (Jude 13). In light of such descriptions it would be well for us to meditate on the subject of hell and allow God to break our hearts with the very thing that breaks his heart – the thousands of souls that every day pass into a Christless eternity.

Charles Spurgeon, the "Prince of Preachers", is not known for his hell-fire sermons, but in one instance he sought to bring a greater awareness of hell to his hearers;

> Your body will be prepared by God in such a way that it will burn for ever without being consumed. With your nerves laid raw by the searing flame, yet never desensitised for all its raging fury and acrid smoke of the sulphurous flames searing your lungs and choking your breath, you will cry out for mercy of death but it will never, no never, no never give you surcease. (Quoted in Jon Braun, *Whatever Happened to Hell*.)

It does not matter whether Spurgeon's opinion is literally true or not, but it should awaken us to the fact that the Bible depicts hell as a place of eternal torment. Descriptions such as outer darkness and black darkness should fill us with a sense of fear for those who are on their way to such a place.

All of us, at some time or another, have been afraid of the dark. Imagine, though, the torment for someone who, in total darkness, remembers his life time (Lk. 16:25), the memories of all the beautiful sights he has seen – the flowers, the sunsets, the faces, and so many other things that come flooding back. He remembers the good times, the bad times, and the times he had the opportunity to receive Christ but rejected him. He realises that for the rest of eternity he will continue to see nothing but darkness, and has nothing to look forward to, nothing to reflect on except his own foolishness in not accepting Christ.

It is said that William Booth, founder of the Salvation Army, wished all officers commissioned under him could hang over hell for twenty-four hours prior to their commissioning. He felt sure this would stir them in a deeper commitment to evangelism. While a greater awareness of hell should not be our primary motive for evangelism, knowing we are delivered from the wrath to come should have a definite place in our theology of missions.

I believe that our supreme motive in reaching the lost should be our love for the Lord, and desire to want to please him. But we also need a revelation of the lostness of the lost, and need continually to ask ourselves if we really believe that our friends, relatives, acquaintances, as well as all unbelievers are for ever lost unless they turn to Christ. The fact that God in his infinite wisdom has laid down a just penalty for sin – eternal separation from him and his life – should motivate us to reach out and love our neighbours as ourselves by sharing the gospel message with them.

The advent of different forms of liberal and modernistic theology has seen the subject of hell slowly lose its sting. Apart from the occasional reference to Jonathan Edwards' *Sinners in the Hands of an Angry God*, or a thumping hell-fire and brimstone message, hell is seldom mentioned from the pulpit. Nowadays, it is most often used as a swear-word, or in jest in careless remarks like, "When I get to hell I'll throw a party because so many of my friends will be there." We must not allow people to make light of such a place, but tell them the folly of their way, being prepared to weep in front of them, if need be, to show them the gravity of the issue.

Leonard Ravenhill tells of Charlie Peace, a convicted criminal sentenced to die by hanging. On his walk to the gallows, the prison chaplain glibly read him some Bible verses from a book called *The Consolation of Religion*. Charlie was shocked that a minister who professed to believe in the Bible could so coldly and professionally read about hell without so much as a tear in his eye or a quiver in his voice. "How can he believe that there is an eternal fire which never consumes its victims and yet be so unmoved?" he mused to himself. Finally, unable to hold his peace any longer, Charlie snapped at the chaplain. "Sir, if I believed what you and the church of God say you believe, even if England were covered with broken glass from coast to coast, I would walk over it, if need be, on hands and knees, and think it worthwhile living, just to save one soul from an eternal hell like that."

As I heard Leonard Ravenhill share this I was cut to the heart, and felt the Holy Spirit challenging me. Paul said, "It is written: 'I believed; therefore I have spoken.' With that same spirit of faith we also believe and therefore speak" (2 Cor. 4:13). It follows then, that if we believe the gospel is God's final word to mankind regarding salvation, then our only right response should be by every means possible to get the news out. Leighton Ford tells of a European Communist who remarked that the only Christian he respected was the one trying to convert him to Christ. We, who are persuaded need also to be *persuaders!*

The work of evangelism is serious business. We are not just trying to give people a new lease on this life by joining our religion, but we are dealing with the issues of life and death, heaven and hell, every time we encounter a non-believer. Paul spoke of having unceasing grief in his heart and wishing he were cut off from Christ for the sake of the lost (Rom. 9:2–3). The Psalmist, also, agonised in his concern for the lost, "Horror has taken hold of me because of the wicked that forsake the law [. . .] Rivers of water run down my eyes" (Psalm 119:53, 136). Jeremiah spoke of sobbing in secret and bitterly weeping over the pride of his people (Jer. 13:17). Many of us find such statements eccentric and extreme, but how can we say they are extreme in the light of the reality of hell? If God would give us half the revelation of the lostness of the lost that these men had, we would be led to fasting, prayer, spiritual warfare, giving and fearless witnessing to see the lost come to Jesus and escape the dangers of a Christless eternity.

After declaring that we all must stand before the judgement seat of Christ, Paul says, "Since then, we know what it is to fear the Lord, we try to persuade men" (2 Cor. 5:11). It is not so much that we need to incorporate hell more into our witnessing, though that may be appropriate at times, but rather we Christians who know the "Fear of the Lord" should be motivated to persuade men. The evangelistic messages of Acts are strangely silent regarding both hell and heaven. I believe this is because God does not want us to use tactics of fear and threat to scare people into salvation, any more than he wants us to use "pie in the sky" to bribe them. Rather, he wants us to present the truth of his death and resurrection (1 Cor. 15:3–4) and let that set men free. The eternal issue of heaven and hell needs mostly to be pressed on *our* minds, as Christians, *so that we see* the gravity and urgency of the matter.

REPENTANCE

"Ye turned to God from idols to serve the living and true God" (1 Thess. 1:9).

Paul understood that becoming a Christian was not just giving "mental assent" to a set of theological creeds.

Rather it meant turning away *from* sin and idolatry (repentance) *to* Jesus Christ (faith), as he summarised to the Ephesian elders; "I have declared to both Jews and Greeks that they must turn to God in repentance and have faith in our Lord Jesus" (Acts 20:21).

Repentance is the first word of the gospel. Jesus said, "Repent, and believe the good news!" (Mark 1:15) and made it clear that his reason for coming was to preach repentance (Lk. 5:32). Likewise he commands us to preach it as well (Lk. 24:47).

True repentance is the natural outworking of true faith. Jesus linked the two very closely when he said the Ninevites had "repented at the preaching of Jonah" (Lk. 11:32). However, the account in the book of Jonah records that they "believed God" (Jonah 3:5) and makes no specific mention of repentance. By inference, we can conclude that repentance and faith are very closely linked and we dare not separate them. The call to faith and the call to repentance are one and the same.

In 1981 two Christians, one an Indian and the other a Chinese Youth With A Mission worker, knocked at a devout young Hindu woman's door. After being invited in they noticed idols everywhere, but undeterred Sam Yeo Le Hok began sharing his testimony, and the gospel. Sashikala, the young Hindu woman, was soon asking what she needed to do to receive salvation, and the two patiently explained her need to repent of sin and receive Christ as her Saviour and Lord. Sashikala understood and was willing to pay the price to follow Jesus completely. Soon a bonfire raged in the backyard as the Hindu deities Shiva, Hanuman and Krishna, along with other idols, were burned.

Dietrich Bonhoeffer, the German theologian, warned of the dangers of offering cheap grace and, on the price God places on his grace, he had this to say:

Such grace is costly because it cost a man his life, and it is grace because it gives him the only true life. It is

costly because it condemns sin, and grace because it
justifies the sinner. Above all, it is costly because it cost
God the life of His son. "Ye are bought with a price,"
and what has cost God so much, cannot be cheap for
us. (Dietrich Bonhoeffer, *The Cost of Discipleship*.)

In our witnessing we must be careful not to com-
promise the gospel message for the sake of increased
numbers of converts. This can happen when we neglect
to preach repentance, and so water down the gospel, and
rob a prospective convert of the joy of sins forgiven. Peter
said, "Repent then, and turn to God, so that your sins
may be wiped out" (Acts 3:19). So, if we turn away from
sin, take up our cross and follow Jesus, he demonstrates
his power to us by giving victory over our sin, and that, in
turn, glorifies him. We rob our hearers of the joy of
victorious Christian living when we neglect to give them
the full gospel. It is true, there will be struggles with
persistent sin, but, as our heart and will is set to follow
Jesus, we soon become victorious.

A word of caution should be added here regarding
"legalism". We must see ourselves as a friend to a new
convert, helping him to repent *from what the Bible says is
sin*, and not trying to mould him to the standards and
beliefs of our particular denomination or group. We all
have a certain "grid", formed by our particular cultural
and denominational environment through which we
view those "grey areas" that the Bible is silent about. We
must be careful, however, that we do not impose our
"grid" on a new convert in place of true biblical repentance, so ensnaring them in a web of legalism. Each new
Christian needs space to develop their own "grid",
which is done as they individually seek God and study
his Word. We must be careful not to preach the doctrines
of men in place of the commandments of God (Matt.
15:9).

The gospel is not man-centred, but God-centred. It
does not revolve around the happiness of man, but the

glory of God. Jesus is not merely a personal Saviour who will meet people's needs. He is the Lord of the universe and demands our full surrender. Without Christ man is an unfortunate creature that God is not obliged to save. By his evil behaviour he has made himself an enemy of God (Col. 1:21) and is under the guilt of his sin. Man deserves judgement, but, by God's mercy and grace, through repentance, he can be forgiven.

LOVING SINNERS

"We loved you so much that we were delighted to share with you not only the gospel of God, but our lives as well, because you had become so dear to us" (1 Thess. 2:8).

If we do not have God's love for the lost, then any evangelistic methods or principles we use will at best be legal stale obedience to a set of commands. The "agape" love of God needs to be the foundation upon which our evangelism is based. Paul writes that even if he abounded in faith, knowledge, spiritual gifts, and good works, but did not have love, then it was all worth nothing (1 Cor. 13:1–3). Jesus said that all men would know we are his disciples by the love we have for each other (John 13:34–5). We must be diligent to make sure that is indeed the case. However, Christians should not be the sole recipients of our love, but also those who desperately need it – the unbelievers. "May the Lord make your love (agape) increase and overflow for each other and for everyone else" (1 Thess. 3:12).

When speaking of love I am not referring to a type of emotional sentimentality, or special way of feeling. God's love is a choice – choosing the highest good of another regardless of our personal feelings. God's feelings towards sinners are recorded in Psalm 7:11: "God [. . .] expresses his wrath every day," but he, ". . .

demonstrates his own love for us in this: While we were still sinners, Christ died for us" (Rom. 5:8). *God chose our highest good above his own feelings.* His loving, merciful response to our sin was the Cross. There are times when unbelievers will not elicit great feelings of love from us, as they speak against the Lord, and reject or persecute us, but, in these situations we must choose to be Christ-like and love them regardless.

An illustration of this kind of love is found in David Wilkerson's book *The Cross and the Switchblade*. Nicky Cruz, a young gang member, threatened to cut David into a thousand pieces. David's response was one of *agape* love, "You cut me into a thousand pieces and every piece will say I love you." Soon afterwards Nicky was converted, and has gone on to preach Christ's love to thousands more.

The fruit of a Spirit-filled life is God's love pouring out of us (Gal. 5:22) to whoever we come in contact with in the course of our day, be they Christian or non-Christian. Regularly we need to be filled with the Holy Spirit, especially when evangelising, where, before approaching someone we need to ask for God's help in truly loving that person. We will be tested at times, but during those times we grow in our capacity to love with God's unconditional love (see Matt. 5:43–8).

As a new Christian, barely a week old in my new faith, my love for the unsaved was severely tested. I was working as a dishwasher in a restaurant, and witnessing to the other employees. One of them, John, the cook, was a member of the church of Satan, and, as I told him about the gospel and the second coming of Christ, he looked at me with evil in his eyes, and let loose a series of horrific remarks against the Lord. One thing he said was, "If Jesus Christ came back to earth right now, and walked into this restaurant, I'd hit him on the head with an axe and pick the worms out of his brain."

Speechless, I fell back against the dishwashing machine. I could not believe anyone could say such foul and demonic things about God. In my silence the Spirit whispered to me, "Danny, do you still love him?" I had to be honest, in my heart I knew I did not. The Lord knew it too, and responded with, "I do!" That day I learned an important lesson – when someone is unlovely, and John was about as unlovely as you could get, God can give us his love for that person. I felt like hitting John with an axe, but God showed me the love he had for him. I wish I could report that John was saved, but I do not know that he ever was. I do know, though, that God is still demonstrating his love towards sinners just like John, and, if we are going to follow in the footsteps of our master, we must do the same.

LIGHT-SHINING EVANGELISM

"And ye became imitators of us and of the Lord" (1 Thess. 1:6).

Jesus spoke of what I call "light-shining evangelism" in his Sermon on the Mount. He instructed us to let men see our good deeds, so they in turn will glorify the Father in heaven (Matt. 5:16). Often, simply helping a non-Christian will open them to the gospel (Titus 2:14). Helping a neighbour paint his house, cut his lawn, even baby-sitting for his children can open his eyes to the "light of the World". "So that you may become blameless and pure, children of God without fault in a crooked and depraved generation, in which *you shine like stars in the universe* as you hold out the word of life" (Phil. 2:15–16).

Paul was confident that his own life reflected the message he preached. He did not preach unattainable theories, but invited people to see them worked out in his own life, confident that he displayed significant victory over the world, the flesh, and the devil. Thus he could boldly tell the Thessalonains, "Follow our example" (2 Thess. 3:7).

A Christ-like example is essential if we are to be effective in evangelism. I have interviewed scores of people who have been brought to salvation by simply seeing the gospel lived out in a person's life. Charles Finney once said, "Christians are the greatest reason for accepting Christ, they are also the greatest excuse not to." Just as, "The Word became flesh and made his dwelling among us" (John 1:14), so today, that Word must be lived out in the lives of those who are his body.

Unfortunately, the bumper sticker, "Christians aren't perfect, just forgiven", seems to more adequately describe the gospel as we represent it to the world. While, in a technical sense, that is true, as none of us are sinlessly perfect, the New Testament also teaches that we are more than merely forgiven. It teaches that we are forgiven *and changed*. Jesus' death was not only to bring forgiveness of sin, but also victory over sin (Rom. 6). By God's grace we can "purify ourselves from everything that contaminates body and spirit, perfecting holiness out of reverence for God" (2 Cor. 7:1). We are partakers of his holiness and divine nature (Heb. 12:10; 2 Peter 1:4) and have been promised that, as a result of the New Covenant, he will give us the power of his Spirit to live and walk victoriously, as we obey him. "I will put my Spirit in you and move you to follow my decrees and be careful to keep my laws" (Ezek. 36:27).

I cannot imagine Paul sheepishly walking up to a fellow tentmaker, head down, and saying, "I'm just as much a wretch as you, but I'm forgiven. Don't look at me, look at Jesus." No, I think he would have witnessed something like this, "I was no good, but Jesus forgave me and changed my life. He gives me power over the world, the flesh, and the devil, because he gave me his Holy Spirit. Follow me, because I'm following Jesus." He would not have been revealing pride in saying this, instead he was giving God the glory for the changes worked in his life. As a song says, "From glory to glory he's changing me, his likeness and image made perfect in me."

Not all of us are Pauls, and the thought of going up to someone we have never met and sharing the gospel with them strikes fear to our heart. Our reply, when confronted with the challenge of a lifestyle of evangelism is, "Well, that's okay for them, they're so outgoing," or, "Yes, I'd like to, but it's just not me. I could never be as bold as that." However, our reaction need not be that way, the nagging fears and doubts can be overcome.

Chapter 4

Fears and attitudes

"Paranoia strikes deep; into your life it will creep; starts when you're always afraid . . ." Though penned by a secular rock musician, these words accurately describe the main (most common?) hindrance to the lifestyle of evangelism – the fear of man. We are warned that "Fear of man will prove to be a snare . . ." (Prov. 29:25) and I am sure each one of us would admit that, at some time or other, this fear has ensnared our witnessing for the Lord.

There are times when I have felt frustrated, backing out when God had led me to witness to someone. In spite of scriptural admonitions not to fear, and that perfect love casts out fear, one way or another fear seemed to cast out my perfect love! There were times when I tried to be "God's man of faith and power", mustering my courage and willpower, but when it came to opening my mouth and witnessing, I could not.

The Lord began to speak to me about specific fears I had, and how to deal with them in the light of his Word. Let us look at some of the most common fears I have discovered, both from my own experience, and from interviewing other Christians in many parts of the world.

Fear of rejection

This is a big fear, especially in the western world. Rejection is hard to handle, even for the most thick-skinned of us, since we have a built-in need for love and acceptance. In witnessing though, we often find people to be neither loving nor accepting, so we must face this fact – *every ambassador for Christ is essentially a rejected person!* Jesus was "despised and rejected by men" (Isa. 53:3). "He came to that which was his own, but his own did not receive him" (John 1:11). "They got up, drove him out of the town . . ." (Luke 4:29); "And when they saw him, they pleaded with him to leave their region" (Matt. 8:34); "But first he must suffer many things and be rejected by this generation" (Luke 17:25). Many accepted Jesus and his message, but more still rejected him, and, if we want to be like him, we must learn to handle this same rejection.

When I teach on evangelism I like to ask, "Do you feel like witnessing on the streets tonight?" Usually, only a small percentage raise their hands, so I go on, "What if I guarantee that tonight every one of you will lead the first person you approach to the Lord, how many would feel like it then?" Almost without fail, every hand will shoot up, because everyone wants themselves, and their message, to be accepted. No one relishes being put down, ignored, or looked upon as a fool.

The key to handling rejection is making sure we are getting all the acceptance we need from the Father, and not looking for it in the world. Evangelism, by its very nature, means we are uninvited people taking an uncomfortable message to a Christ-rejecting world where many will not accept it. However, the glorious good news is that some will receive it if we go out fearlessly, trusting that the perfect love of Jesus will cast out fear. Scripture tells us, "He who fears the Lord has a secure fortress, and for his children it will be a refuge. The fear of the Lord is a fountain of life, turning a man from the snares of death" (Prov. 14:26–7). If we look to the Lord for our acceptance, placing our identity in him, and standing in awe of who he is, then the snare of the fear of man will fall away. Jesus said, "Do not be afraid of those who kill the body but cannot kill the soul; rather, be afraid of the one who can destroy both soul and body in hell" (Matt. 10:28). So we must be more concerned about what God thinks than what men think. We will be rejected by some, scorned and put down by others, but we must not be concerned with whether the unbeliever will reject us, and instead tell him that he will not be rejected by God because of his sin – if he repents of it.

Fear of losing reputation

The way to deal with this is easy – give up your reputation! Jesus made himself of no reputation (Phil. 2:7) so that, when he was shamefully nailed to the cross, he had no reputation to lose. Our identity must be based in Jesus, and not on our reputation in the world, whatever that may be. Too many Christians never experience victory in this area simply because they continue basing their identity on something other than the Lord. If our identity is found in being a rational level-headed person, then we will be tempted not to be too radical in our witness for fear we will be thought of as a religious fanatic. The same is true of our reputation at work, in school, with peers, and the like. I once saw a T-shirt that said, "I'm a fool for Christ, whose fool are you?" and, while we should not *try* to be foolish, we must remember that the gospel message we preach sounds like foolishness to the natural mind (1 Cor. 1:18). Once and for all we must settle where our identity and reputation lies. As Paul said, "May I never boast except in the cross of our Lord Jesus Christ, through which the world has been crucified to me, and I to the world" (Gal. 6:14).

Fear of physical harm

I have talked with Christians from Muslim countries whose lives have literally become endangered simply because they are Christians. Jesus warned there would be a time when Christians would be killed by people who thought they were doing God a favour, a fact borne out thousands of times throughout history. Our fear of rejection and losing reputation seems trifling when compared to Christians in some parts of the world who literally fear for their lives every time they witness to someone, or hold a Bible study. We in the western world need to learn a lesson from these Christians, since the Bible nowhere says that we are exempt from physical harm or death for preaching the Gospel: ". . . everyone who wants to live a godly life in Christ Jesus will be persecuted" (2 Tim. 3:12). We must ask God for the faith and strength to stand firm in the face of any and every fear, be it physical, mental, emotional, or spiritual, which Satan may throw at us. Remember Paul's words, "I have been crucified with Christ, and I no longer live, but Christ lives in me. The life I now live in the body I live by faith in the Son of God, who loved me and gave himself for me" (Gal. 2:20).

Fear of being inadequate

Here we feel we do not know enough to answer all the questions an unbeliever may ask of us, and some do ask difficult questions. Some ask questions looking for an argument, while others, often spiritually hungry, are looking for earnest answers. We need to be sensitive to this, so that we do not become embroiled in arguments with people who are wasting our time, and neglect to give honest answers to those who *are* spiritually hungry. After all, they are the people who deserve honest answers to their questions, and we must be prepared to give them. We must realise, though, that as we grow daily in our knowledge of God, we are never going to have all the answers to all the questions asked of us. When we do not know the answer to a question, we must be prepared to do some homework and search it out, and

afterwards we can arrange to meet the person who asked
the question and discuss the answer. Researching in this
way has a triple benefit. Firstly, it shows the person we
care about them and their question. Secondly, by their
willingness to meet and discuss at a later time we can
measure their sincerity in asking the question, and
thirdly, we grow in our knowledge and ability to answer
the same question should someone else ask it in the
future. We are exhorted by Peter to "Always be prepared
to give an answer to everyone who asks you to give a
reason for the hope that you have. But do this with
gentleness and respect . . ." (1 Pet. 3:15).

One thing to keep in mind is that even when we do not
know the answer to a difficult question a non-Christian
may ask, we do know Jesus, and can testify to what he
has done in our lives. The woman at the well is an
example of this. Barely one day old in her faith, she
testified and led many of her fellow Samaritans to Christ
(Jn. 4:39).

There are other fears that could be listed and ex-
pounded upon here, but most fall into the above four
categories. When we experience any type of fear in
evangelism we must deal with it, otherwise it will cripple
our witness for Jesus. We must not allow Satan to condemn us because of our fears, for if that happens we will
never see any hope for being free of them. Instead we
must be honest with God and ourselves about our fears.
We can learn a lesson in this regard from the early
church, whose prayer, in the midst of great suffering and
persecution, was "Now, Lord, consider their threats,
and enable your servants to speak your word with great
boldness . . . After they prayed . . . they were all filled
with the Holy Spirit and spoke the word of God boldly"
(Acts 4:29–31).

We should not be discouraged if we never completely
conquer all of these fears, but as we submit to Jesus and
love him we will begin to experience a substantial
amount of victory over them. As we trust in God's

character and continually place our trust in him, our faith will be the victory that overcomes anything the world can throw at us, *including* the fear of man (1 Jn. 5:4–5). Note David's encouraging formula for victory over fear, "God is our refuge and strength, an ever-present help in trouble. *Therefore we will not fear* though the earth give way, and though the mountains fall into the heart of the sea" (Psalm 46:1–2).

HAVING THE RIGHT ATTITUDE

"Your attitude should be the same as that of Christ Jesus; Who, being in very nature God, did not consider equality with God something to be grasped, but made himself nothing, taking the very nature of a servant, and being made in human likeness" (Phil. 2:5–7).

Most unbelievers can easily pick up a bad attitude in a person witnessing to them. Self-righteousness, hypocrisy, pride and many other bad attitudes are easily spotted by non-Christians. In evangelism our attitude must be the foundation for our actions, and "When the foundations are being destroyed, what can the righteous do?" (Psalm 11:3). Often we are ineffective in communicating the gospel not because we do not say the right things, but because we say the right things with the wrong attitude. Speech teachers tell us that *how* you say something will get more response than the actual content of what you say.

1. Do not be self-righteous

"It is because of him you are in Christ Jesus, now become for us wisdom from God – that is, our righteousness, holiness and redemption. Therefore, as it is

written: 'Let him who boasts, boast in the Lord'" (1 Cor.
1:30–1).

Evangelism has been described as one beggar telling
another where he can find bread. We are only made
righteous in Jesus Christ, and not by our works, no
matter how sanctified we think ourselves to be. The very
reason most people are lost is because most people are
self-righteous. We must not allow ourselves to come
across to people in this way, or we will be presenting the
gospel in a wrong spirit. We must lift up Jesus as the
author and finisher of our faith, and let Him draw men to
Himself.

2. Do not be hypocritical

We must live out what we profess to believe so that the
name Christian becomes synonymous with a quality of
living that truly reflects the character of Jesus. What we
need is more biblical living, not more biblical talking. We
must walk in holiness, and trust in God's grace to overcome sin and hypocrisy in our lives.

3. Do not be critical

Several years ago I grew cold in my relationship with the
Lord, and it showed itself in a lack of joy and faith, a
growing legalism, and absence of fruit in my evangelism.
In the midst of this God revealed to me that I had
developed a critical spirit, and that my judging of others
was having severe repercussions in every area of my
Christian life. I repented of pride, the root of the problem
and, by the grace of God, was restored.

In the midst of this situation God showed me a vision
in which I was working on an assembly line. As long as I
kept my eyes fixed on the work I was doing on the
assembly line, the work got done. But, when I began

looking around at what others were doing on the assembly line, my work did not get done. From this I learned that, to the extent that I spend my time criticising and judging others, to that same extent my work, which God has specifically given me to do, will not get done. These words of Jesus need to be the rule we live by, "I did not come to judge the world, but to save it" (John 12:47).

Evangelist Arthur Blessitt, while hanging on his twelve-foot cross on Sunset Strip, led an acquaintance of mine to the Lord, and, at a wild party, another friend was saved when he forgot to turn off the television set that was airing a Billy Graham broadcast. Other people have been converted at Christian rock concerts, in bars, churches, coffee houses, on the streets, the beach, at home, and in a myriad other such places. God will use any and every means possible, even things we may personally not agree with, to bring people to himself. We must make sure we are doing what he has called us to do, and not spending our time criticising the means he has instructed others to use.

Having a clean spirit is essential to having an evangelistic lifestyle. Many evangelists may not do things the way we would like them to be done – we need to be praying that God will bless their ministry. Paul rejoiced that the gospel was being preached, even when it was done out of a motive of envy or strife (Phil. 1:15–18). Many unorthodox means of preaching the gospel have been used in the last two thousand years, and many more will be tried in the future, but, as Paul said – do it by all means possible (1 Cor. 9:22).

Rather than allowing a critical spirit to develop, always keep in mind these words: "Each one should test his own actions. Then can take pride in himself, without comparing himself to somebody else" (Gal. 6:4). Likewise John says, "Watch out that you do not lose what you have worked for" (2 Jn. 8).

4. Do not see people as statistics

We should not just be buttonholing non-believers in order to chalk up another soul for Christ. Instead we should be genuinely concerned for the welfare of the person we are witnessing to. The seemingly righteous, "God said it, take it or leave it, turn or burn" posture many Christians adopt in their witnessing is more effective in turning people off the gospel than on to it. A caring relationship needs to grow with the person, as we love them with God's love – people do not really care how much we know, until they know how much we care! Our love for the lost, not just in word, but in action and deed, is the foundation upon which evangelism is built (1 Jn. 3:17–18).

HORSES AND MULES

"Do not be like the horse or the mule, which have no understanding, but must be controlled by bit and bridle" (Psalm 32:9).

The horse and the mule, I believe, can represent two different types of Christians, and how they approach witnessing. The horse represents the zealous, aggressive type of Christian, whose zeal for evangelism calls to mind the image of a frisky thoroughbred waiting at the starting gate for the Derby to begin. This type of Christian will witness to anyone and everyone, whether God tells them to or not. They do not like to beat around the bush, but get straight to the point with the non-Christian. Their zeal and fire for God is commendable, but needs to be tempered with a broken and contrite spirit, or their natural aggressiveness, which God gave them as a strength, can quickly turn to self-confidence, self-sufficiency, pride, and a critical spirit toward others who do not have the same "zeal".

The mule, by contrast, represents the soft-spoken, passive type of Christian. Whereas the horse will witness at the drop of a hat, the mule often needs visions, dreams, prophecies, angels singing and bells ringing before he will "feel led" to share his faith. He needs a good kick in the hind parts to get moving into the harvest field for Jesus. Horses and mules need each other in evangelism and often the Lord will give us the opposite type to be our witnessing partner so we can be balanced. God wants to deliver us from both unrestrained zeal and apathetic indifference so we will listen to His voice and be obedient as we go out to share the good news. We can learn a lesson from the example of a horse named Peter, and a mule named Jonah, who learned their lessons the hard way.

It is not overcoming our fears and having the right attitudes alone that make us a good evangelist, though they help. It is being sensitive to God's voice and witnessing when and where he tells us to, be it work, home, our sports club, the streets, or any place people are, that makes us effective witnesses.

Just as in fishing, you fish where the fish are, it is the same for today's "fishers of men".

Chapter 5

Witnessing where the people are

Once, as I witnessed outside a bar, a man got very upset with me and, amidst four-letter words, told me the place for religion was in the church and I should keep my message there. I told him I would like to, except for the fact that most people do not go to church! Evangelism is not for the church, and if we want to reach sinners we must go where they are – on the street, in bars, their homes, on the job, and the like. Jesus told us to go into all the world, not the church, and preach the gospel. When challenged by the Pharisees as to why he ate and drank with tax collectors and sinners Jesus replied, "I have not come to call the righteous, but sinners to repentance" (Luke 5:32). The church is the place for *teaching* the Word of God, not preaching, so that those taught might be equipped to minister to a lost world – right where they are.

WITNESSING WHERE YOU ARE

"Preach the Word, be prepared in season and out of season . . ." (2 Tim. 4:2).

Early in my walk with the Lord I had a desire to witness, but I did not really know how, and kept asking the Lord for the right atmosphere, situation, and timing.

Sometimes I found that witnessing flowed smoothly, and at others it just did not go quite right at all and those "in season" opportunities for witnessing did not seem to come often enough. Then, I discovered Paul's exhortation to his young disciple Timothy to be ready in season and out. The Greek words for "in season and out of season" can be translated "conveniently and inconveniently". So, there are times when it is more convenient to witness than others, but just because it is inconvenient does not mean the Spirit does not want us to share. A good rule to follow in this is to presume God wants us to share the gospel with everyone, unless he leads otherwise. After all, he has already told us to tell "every creature" and will prepare a way for us to do just that.

Since becoming a Christian, I have worked in a restaurant, a cannery, on a Christmas tree farm, as a construction labourer and cement finisher, and in "full-time" ministry. In each of these situations I have had many opportunities to be God's missionary to the people I worked with. Sometimes it was convenient to share, other times it was not, but his promise was always there to keep me going, "My word [. . .] will not return to me empty, but will accomplish what I desire" (Isa. 55:11).

When I was about six months old in my relationship with the Lord, I worked at a spinach cannery, and while I did not know many Bible verses, I had a story to tell. I was rejected by many as I tried to share the good news with them, but some, like Lorraine, did not. She was a streetwise young woman who came to work every day with a switchblade in her pocket, and a tough boyfriend named Louie. Both rejected the Lord at first, Louie even threatening to stab me, but, to make a long story short, Lorraine got saved while Louie got fired! Today Lorraine sings for an Assembly of God choir.

On the cannery assembly line Norman and I worked together. He argued with me for weeks about the irrelevance of the gospel, and how he believed all roads led to

God. But God got him before the spinach season was over, and today he's a firefighter for Christ!

Eileen worked further along the same assembly line and used to ask me questions about God and the Bible during our ten-minute breaks. Many of her questions I could not answer straight away and so would have to do some homework. Eileen eventually gave her life to Jesus as well.

Pat Brown threw the tract I gave her on the ground in disgust. Later, though, she accepted Jesus as her Lord, and is actively involved in a Pentecostal church today. Janice, at first, covered her emptiness by rejecting my witness, but later, I also had the privilege of leading her to Christ and baptising her. She is now serving the Lord in Minnesota.

These are my spinach cannery stories, and they could be echoed thousands of times over by many other Christians, in various jobs around the world, who witness right where they are. Your job, family, neighbourhood, and the like are ready-made situations God has placed you in to be his witness. We do not need to wait for dreams, visions, ringing bells, or audible voices before we start sharing our faith. We are already called to abide in Christ and be active witnesses for him wherever he has placed us (1 Cor. 7:24). Some people are mistakenly waiting to be sent to the mission field before they witness regularly and are missing out on so many glorious opportunities of leading people to a relationship with Jesus Christ. Step out in faith and witness today – right where you are!

THE "DIVINE APPOINTMENT"

As we continue to walk with the Lord, we grow in our ability to be sensitive to his leading in our life, both in the day-to-day matters, and when we are out sharing our faith with others. It is a good practice to schedule a time into our weekly routine that we use specifically for sharing the good news about Jesus with the lost. We schedule and discipline every other area of our life – going to work, recreation, entertainment, Bible studies, prayer meetings, and so on. So, why not schedule a weekly time to spend with non-Christians in whatever type of outreach or friendship evangelism that seems applicable. Don't just passively wait for it to happen, but *passionately pursue* "divine appointments" that the Holy Spirit arranges in the course of our day. Often we are so engrossed in our daily affairs that "divine appointments" just seem like another interruption. So, we must be alert and actively seeking them.

On a recent plane trip an elderly man sat next to me. I was physically tired and not really in the mood for witnessing, but before long had struck up a conversation with him. Soon he was pouring his heart out to me in regard to his health, having recently been diagnosed with terminal cancer, and given only three months to live. I asked him about his relationship to God and he admitted that his recent diagnosis had awakened a spiritual hunger within him. On that flight I had the privilege of leading him to Christ. It was a "divine appointment", and even though I had not been looking for it, God had arranged it – after all, he is in control of my schedule!

· Petrus, a young man from Micronesia, was waiting at a local street corner for the crossing light to change when Mike and I met him. I pulled a gospel tract out and began talking to him about his spiritual life, inviting him to a coffee house to continue the conversation. After about ten minutes he told us that just three days earlier he had asked God to reveal himself, and now marvelled at the "coincidence" of meeting Mike and me. Several other coincidences also just seemed to line up, such as his brother's house, where he was staying, being right across the street from the church I was to be preaching at that Sunday, which was also close to where I lived so I could follow him up. Petrus went back to Micronesia a changed man, all because of a "divine appointment".

Early in 1986, a young couple from the Gospel Outreach church in Springfield, Oregon, were having a mediocre day of door-to-door evangelism. Shortly before they decided to stop for the day they were invited into the house of a young lady who seemed open to the gospel. On a subsequent visit they were able to lead her to the Lord, and she later explained that at the very moment they knocked at her door on their first visit she had a pistol at her head, trying to muster the courage to pull the trigger. By "divine appointment" two willing workers were able to give her eternal life instead of a bullet in the head!

Goutam was a young radical from the Communist-governed state of West Bengal, India. While on a train from Calcutta to his home town of Uluberia, he "just happened" to sit next to two Youth With A Mission workers who diligently shared the gospel with him. Over the next few days following the encounter he began to see the emptiness of his Communist ideology and came to believe that Jesus was the answer to the emptiness he was feeling. He turned his life over to God and became a radical for Jesus! Today, he is involved in church planting in northern India and attributes his conversion to the "perfectly timed" divine appointment on a train bound for glory!

"Divine appointments" sometimes come as the result of random encounters, and when we least expect them. At other times we will feel a spiritual inclination to approach someone with a question, maybe a word of wisdom, or knowledge that God has given us for them. Regardless of how an encounter happens, we need to be expecting the unexpected to happen, then we begin to see those "interruptions" that beset us in the course of our day as ordained of God to bring someone into his kingdom. In this way every day becomes an adventure as God begins to arrange our circumstances for his glory!

THE WITNESSING DIALOGUE –
A HEARING EAR

"The sovereign Lord has given me an instructed tongue, that I should know the word that sustains the weary. He wakens me morning by morning, wakens my ear to listen like one being taught" (Isa. 50:4).

In personal evangelism it is important that we do not seek so much to preach *at* people, as to talk *to* them about a relationship with Jesus Christ. Talking implies that we have dialogue with a person, and in dialogue listening is just as important as speaking. We must learn to listen as well as talk in our conversations with people about the Lord. Jesus' method of evangelism usually centred around asking questions, listening to the reply and responding to it with the words of life. By listening he understood that the woman of Samaria needed living water, and that Nicodemus needed to hear about being born again. He was able to respond to their area of need – because he listened. Often we will not discover a person's area of need until we start asking them questions and sensitively listen to their answers, which requires discipline as the tendency is to be thinking of the next thing we are going to say while the other person is talking. We know that everyone needs to be saved, but the real issue is, how do we most effectively present Christ in a particular situation? After all, we are not selling salvation-in-a-can, but are presenting a *personal* Lord and Saviour who is able to meet the individual's need. We can effectively do this by really listening and hearing what they are saying, while at the same time expecting them to listen patiently as we respond to what they have said.

Recently, while witnessing on Union Square in San Francisco, a young man started telling me why he could not be saved, going on and on with the standard excuses – too many hypocrites, the Bible is a myth, what about all

the pygmies in Africa, and so on. I sat listening for about
twenty minutes and began wondering if I was just wasting time, when I heard the Spirit whisper to me, "Just
hear him out." After another forty-five minutes of ram-
blings he went off to buy some cigarettes, inviting me to
go with him to the bar for a drink. When I accepted his
invitation he seemed a little shocked, but, while I sipped
my coke, he began pouring out his heart, the hurts and
fears that had plagued him all his life. He literally cried in
his beer as I shared the gospel with him, urging him to
give his life to the Lord. He did not, but left that bar
promising me he would give serious consideration to
receiving Jesus.

Sometimes we need to earn the right to speak to a
person by giving them a hearing ear. This takes time, but
if we really love people as Jesus did we will take that time
– people are worth it!

INTEREST DOORS

Using an "interest door" means simply taking advantage
of a common interest you may have with an unbeliever,
through which you can share the gospel. Jesus, for
example, used water as an "interest door" to show the
woman at the well her need for living water (Jn. 4). Paul
used the altar to the Unknown God and some Greek
poetry as an "interest door" through which to share the
gospel with the philosophers of Mars Hill (Acts 17:22
–31). An "interest door" allows the Holy Spirit to take an
everyday topic and use it as an opportunity to share the
gospel message. For instance, in 1983 there was a TV
film, *The Day After*, that depicted the aftermath of a
nuclear war. It was soon the topic of everyone's conversation, since the film ended with two men, totally
without hope, crying on each other's shoulder, leaving

the eighty million Americans who watched it with the same hopeless feeling. It provided an "interest door" through which to share the hope that is in Christ, and many Christians took advantage of it.

We need to be informed as to what is happening in our world, since local and world news, politics, economics, entertainment, and even sports are all effective "interest doors". As we share, we also need to be praying that our topical approach will spark interest in an unbeliever's heart, so that we can go on and present the gospel to them.

One afternoon recently, after teaching at a church in California, I picked up a hitch-hiker as I drove through town. As we rode on down the street I noticed that on the front of his cap he had the logo of the rock group "Black Sabbath", a group known for its satanic overtones. I asked him if he liked the group, and he responded, "Yeah." "Aren't they into the devil?" I went on. "That's what I heard," he replied, so I asked him, "Are you into the devil?" He told me he was not, he just liked the group's music. "Well, I'm into God!" I told him, and spent about twenty minutes, sitting in the car in front of his house, talking with him and giving my testimony. He opened up and began to tell me of some deep needs he had in his life. He had just been sentenced to four months in prison for some crimes he had committed, and so I was able to arrange for members of the church to keep in touch with him. Soon they were busy studying the Bible with him in the prison. It started with giving him a lift (Matt. 5:16) then using his love of rock music as an "interest door" through which to share the gospel.

I was the guest speaker at some outreach meetings in California that several churches were holding in a tent at a local park. While preparing for one of my messages I felt distinctly impressed by the Lord to include an illustration from Peter Stoner's book *Science Speaks*. The illustration had to do with the statistical probability of one man fulfilling the Old Testament prophecies relating to the

Messiah. (Stoner had calculated the odds of one individual fulfilling just eight prophecies as equivalent to covering the entire state of Texas two feet deep in silver dollars and then asking a blindfolded man to pull out the one specially marked coin on his first try. Jesus actually fulfilled over three hundred prophecies which of course raises the odds to the almost unbelievable!) Jim, a student at a local junior college, attended the service in which I shared the illustration. At the end of the service I gave an invitation for those present to receive Christ, and Jim responded.

Six months later I met Jim at a church where I was preaching and he shared his story with me. "I wasn't necessarily interested in spiritual things, but had some free time that night and so I went to the tent meeting. I happened to be studying the science of compound probability in one of my classes at the time so your illustration about the prophecies awakened my interest enough to consider seriously who Jesus claimed to be. By the time you reached the altar call I had made my decision."

Jim had responded to the gospel because as it was shared through an "interest door" that was relevant, personal and applied to him at the time. I believe I received a "Word in Season" (Isa. 50:4) about what Jim needed to hear. God is faithful to give us the wisdom that it takes to win souls (Prov. 11:30) and at times, as in Jim's case, He gives a preacher a "word" in a message for many that was especially aimed at an individual.

OUT ON THE STREETS

"Then our sons in their growth will be like well-nurtured plants, and our daughters will be like pillars carved to adorn a palace. Our barns will be filled with every kind of provision. Our sheep will increase by thousands, by tens of thousands in our fields" (Psalm 144:12–13).

Youth With A Mission runs a street ministry on Hotel Street, in the red-light district of Honolulu. I was witnessing to one of the regulars recently and he asked me why church people would be in such an apparently God-forsaken place as Hotel Street. Without thinking I replied, "You know, if Jesus were to come to town, this is probably the place he would visit first." As I reflected on this I realised the real truth of it, Jesus did not come to call the righteous, but sinners to repentance (Luke 5:32), so Hotel Street is as high on his priority list as any other street. I believe God can use us to bring many souls into his kingdom, right on the street. After all, Jesus and the apostles took their message to the streets, and he has told us to go into the streets and alleys of the city and compel people to come to him (Luke 14:23).

One of the things I enjoy about cities is the bustle of people that I can talk to about Jesus. As I witness to a person on the street and find my message rejected, immediately I can go to another, and another, until I find someone who wants to hear about Jesus. If you have never witnessed on the streets before, team up with someone who has experience of it, and get your feet wet – you will be glad you did!

STREET WITNESSING – THE APPROACH

How do I approach a total stranger on the street and begin talking to him about Jesus? This is the dilemma many Christians find themselves in when beginning street witnessing. To be honest, I have not found many suave, debonair ways of breaking into conversation about Jesus with a person on the street. Most people are not on the street just waiting for someone to come up and

tell them about Jesus, so there is bound to be a little
awkwardness, no matter how good the approach we use.

The first thing that we must do is believe God has
prepared the way before us, "If the Lord delights in a
man's way, he makes his steps firm" (Psalm 37:23). Even
the rejections we encounter will be used by God to spur
us on to a fruitful witnessing experience. Be looking for
"divine appointments" and asking God to show us the
right "interest door" through which to share the gospel
on the street. The "interest door" approach will make the
transition from the natural to the spiritual easier.

Recently, in Waikiki, I noticed a street vendor selling
pearls in the oyster to passing tourists. I walked over to
him and asked, "Have you ever heard of the pearl of
great price?" Astonished, he looked at me and told me he
had not, so I used the opening to share Jesus' story of the
pearl merchant with him. I went on to tell him all I knew
the Bible had to say on pearls – the pearly gates, not to
cast your pearl before swine, and so forth. When I could
see he was tiring of hearing about biblical pearls I asked
him to share about pearls in the oyster with me. He did,
and before long the conversation was back around to the
gospel and we talked for another forty-five minutes. It all
started through a pearly "interest door"!

On the street people are often in a hurry, so I have
found being direct a good approach. Do not be afraid to
be honest about why you are there, and trust that God
has prepared the way before you. Often I will use a
gospel tract and approach a person with a smile, saying,
"Could I just give you this to read?" or, "Would you like
some good news," even, "Did you know Jesus loves
you?" There are times when I do not even use a tract, but
just approach someone and ask for a few minutes of their
time to share something important with them. One
advantage of being direct is that if a person does not want
to hear what you have to say they can tell you right at the
outset, so you can find someone who *does* want to hear
and not waste each other's time.

Campus Crusade, Evangelism Explosion, Christian Equippers and other groups have used various surveys and questionnaires as a way of breaking into conversation. Questions such as, "If you were to die tonight, do you have the assurance you would go to heaven?" and, "Who in your opinion was Jesus Christ?" have been used as effective means to open up fruitful conversations about Christ. Remember, in witnessing you must be comfortable with the approach you choose.

STREET PREACHING

"What I tell you in the dark, utter in the daylight; and what is whispered in your ear proclaim from the roofs" (Matt. 10:27).

When I first became a Christian, street preaching was last on my list of priorities in serving God. The stereotype of a "gloom and doom", hell-fire preacher, scowl on his face, holding a sandwich board and wearing sackcloth and ashes while screaming at people to repent, was not something I wanted to be a part of. Not that I had anything against preaching, but simply, most street preachers I had ever seen looked as though they had come from another planet! As I began to study the scriptures, though, I noticed that open-air preaching was often mentioned, and began to realise it had a valid place in today's world. It was then that the Lord spoke to my heart, "Okay Danny, since you think street preachers are weird, you go and preach on the streets, *without* being weird!"

There are times when street preaching is not appropriate, and we must be sensitive to the Lord, while at the same time using our common sense. In my own evangelism on the streets I have found the one-to-one conversation approach to be the most fruitful. But there are crowded streets, parks and squares, especially in the city, that are conducive to open-air rallies and house-top type preaching, where a large number of people can be reached in a short amount of time. Music, street drama and mime often help in drawing a crowd before the gospel is preached. Groups such as Open Air Campaigners have incorporated sketchboard sermons, rope tricks, and flash-cards into their presentation of the gospel. While some object to the use of such gimmicks, we must remember that, when we are on the streets, we need to be creative. People are not walking around on the streets with hymnals in hand waiting for church to start! The issue in any method of evangelism is communication. Are we communicating the gospel effectively? Methods that worked twenty years ago may not work today, and methods that work in Bangkok may not work in Chicago. We must be creative and flexible, always open to the guidance of the Lord of the Harvest.

LITERATURE EVANGELISM

We have yet to realise the full value of the printed page. With little money and only a handful of committed workers we can saturate large populations with gospel literature. Scores of people have come to know the Lord through gospel books and tracts.

My first exposure to Jesus Christ came in 1972 on a Californian beach. Someone handed me a copy of the *Hollywood Free Paper*, a gospel tabloid published during the "Jesus movement", and which contained testimonies of champion surfers who had recently become Christians. These spoke to my heart, and it was soon afterwards that my life was radically changed.

Throughout history Christians have made valuable use of the printed page, John Wesley founded Britain's first tract society, while Luther, Calvin and other reformers reached millions through their tracts. William Carey shook the evangelical world of his day with the widely publicised tract, *An Inquiry into the Obligation of Christians to use Means for the Conversion of the Heathen*, while George Verwer, founder of Operation Mobilisation, was converted after someone sent him a gospel of John in the post.

Today, groups such as Last Days Ministries, the American Tract Society and Good News Underground offer tracts and materials free of charge, and we would do well to take advantage of all that these paper missionaries have to offer us. It was Karl Marx who remarked that the short pamphlet is the most powerful of all revolutionary tools and, according to Mahatma Gandhi's nephew in India, "The missionaries taught us to read, but the Communists gave us the literature." Such a comment should stir us to fill the world with gospel literature.

Literature evangelism, like mass evangelism and street preaching, has some inherent weaknesses. For example, it is not as personal as a conversation, and a gospel tract cannot disciple anyone. However, passing out tracts on the street, or distributing them to people we meet in the course of our day, can be a stepping stone to developing boldness in witnessing. It is easier, when starting out, to pass out gospel literature rather than going straight into a witnessing conversation. Remember, literature has the power to speak to a person's heart and open up a door to share more later, through conversation.

I have found writing my own gospel tracts to be effective. I first started doing this because at times I felt uncomfortable with the particular tracts that were available. I was never comfortable with the "Frankenstein" type – the sort with a cover cartoon of a person screaming out in agony from the flames of hell. I felt I could avoid this type of excess by writing my own tracts and in general have found people more receptive to them, as I am giving them something that *I* have written. There is also something more personal about handing out your own tract, it is an expression of you and your heart on paper. You may like to consider writing your own tract and having it printed. You can have a thousand copies type-set and printed for less than fifty pounds. Remember, keep it short and to the point. If no ideas seem particularly appropriate then write down your testimony, put your picture on the front of it, passport style, but smiling, and call it "My Story" or something similar. Be sure to include your name and phone number on the back, so people can contact you personally if they want to know more. Be creative, but remember – keep it simple.

Christian books are another tool to use in literature evangelism, and countless numbers of people have been converted through reading them. After reading *Mere Christianity* by C. S. Lewis, Chuck Colson describes leaning on the steering wheel of his car and crying like a baby under conviction of sin. Through the book the Holy Spirit had been able to pin-point the sin of pride in his heart, and soon afterwards he surrendered his life to Christ. Many contemporary books have been used to draw people to the Lord.

DOOR-TO-DOOR EVANGELISM

"I have not hesitated to preach anything that would be helpful to you, but have taught you publicly and from house to house. I have declared to both Jews and Greeks that they must turn to God in repentance, and have faith in our Lord Jesus Christ" (Acts 20:20–1).

Recently, a girl from one of our Youth With A Mission door-to-door witnessing teams came to me rather distressed after an afternoon of house-to-house visitation. She had spent two and a half hours with a Filipino family who had become Jehovah's Witnesses. Knowing that

Filipinos are predominantly Catholic, I asked how it was that this family had joined the Watchtower. I could have put the words in her mouth before she answered. They had been faithfully attending the Catholic church they were raised in until about three years ago, when two Jehovah's Witnesses knocked on their door. The two were very persuasive and promptly seduced the family into joining one of the nation's largest cults.

I used to look on door-to-door evangelism with disdain, since Jehovah's Witnesses, Mormons and other cults all engaged in it, and I did not want to be linked with them. I started to see, though, that I was playing right into the devil's hand, that all over the world thousands of unsuspecting people are being deceived and led astray in their own living rooms. This should provoke us to get to the door *before* the cults. Today, many who are in the Jehovah's Witnesses and the Mormon Church could very well have been won to the body of Christ, had we reached the door first.

The cults go door-to-door to earn their salvation by doing good works. How much more should we, who have salvation by grace, offer this grace with at least the same zeal that the cults display. Jesus said, "I have come to bring fire on the earth, and how I wish it were already kindled" (Luke 12:49).

Listed below are some guide-lines to remember when engaging in door-to-door evangelism:

1. Go out in pairs, ideally a man and a woman, or husband and wife team.
2. Be respectful – remember you are on someone's private property. Do not walk on the lawn, hop the fence, or snoop around the house before knocking on the door.
3. When you have knocked or rung the door-bell, take a step backwards so as not to appear pushy. If no one is at home leave some gospel literature, with a contact number, in the door.
4. Smile, be pleasant and relaxed, and introduce yourself

and say where you are from (First Baptist, Youth With A Mission, neighbourhood Bible study, or the like) and why you are at their door. As in street witnessing, some have used surveys and questionnaires as conversation openers, and if you feel comfortable with this, go for it! If not, ask if you can have a few minutes of their time to share the gospel. It is at this introductory stage that we often get the most nervous.

Bruce and Lucy, for example, were going door-to-door in Sydney, Australia. Bruce was so nervous that when he introduced himself at the door he said, "Hi, *I'm Lucy and this is Bruce*, and we'd like to share the good news of Jesus with you!" The man at the door laughed and decided that if they were willing to go witnessing being that nervous, then they must have something worth listening to. He invited them in, and later invited Jesus into his life.

5. If invited in accept the hospitality graciously. It is often good to compliment them on something in their house, a picture, furniture, or something of that nature, as this helps break the ice and relax both parties. Begin to ask questions and develop a dialogue that will get the person thinking about their relationship with God.

If the television is on politely ask if they can turn it down a little, and often they will turn it off. If they have small children one of you could entertain them in another part of the room so they will not be a distraction. Be careful not to take them out of sight, or the parents may worry about their safety with a stranger.

If a person becomes uncomfortable during the course of the conversation you should, unless you discern their discomfort is the result of the conviction of sin, excuse yourself politely. Thank them for their time and ask if they would be interested in a further talk. If so, arrange a specific time, at *their convenience*, in the not too distant future. If they are not interested, leave some good gospel literature and a contact phone number, preferably your own. Remember, you only asked for a few moments of their time – do not wear out your welcome!

6. If not invited into the house, politely ask if there is a more convenient time for you to call. If not, try and leave some literature. Remember, always be respectful, polite and loving.

7. Be organised. Keep good records so you can efficiently follow up and go back and contact those who were not at home.

CREATIVE EVANGELISM

There are many methods for sharing the gospel. Our God is creative and we are "partakers of his divine nature" (2 Peter 1:4). So we share his creativity. While much could be discussed here, it will be limited to two major areas — music and drama.

Gospel music

William Booth, founder of the Salvation Army, used to put Christian lyrics to the popular pub tunes of his day, which his Hallelujah Lassies would sing on the streets to share the gospel. This led to accusations of worldliness, but Booth's simple defence was, "Why should the devil have all the good tunes?" Throughout history, from King David to Keith Green, contemporary music has been used to express God's heart of compassion.

Without getting into a debate on rock music, let me say that, in order to communicate, music must be accepted and appreciated by the ears that hear it. Parents often accuse their children of not being able to appreciate good music, while failing to realise that the definition of "good" music changes from generation to generation. The issue to consider when evaluating gospel music, is not whether the beat is syncopated, or how loud it is, but rather whether it is being used by the Holy Spirit, and communicating the gospel. Have people been saved, blessed and brought closer to Jesus as a result of a particular type of contemporary gospel music? If they have, then use it for the glory of God! (see 1 Thess. 5:21)

Jesus said, "For I did not come to judge the world, but to save it" (John 12:47). That should be our motto. I have seen Christian rock bands win hundreds to Christ, and we must continually utilise the kind of music that will relate to contemporary people in today's society if we want to see many brought into the kingdom of God. Be sensitive with the use of music in evangelism and be on the lookout for Christian concerts that you can take a non-Christian friend to, or contemporary albums you could give them.

Gospel drama

Gospel drama can range from puppets in child evangelism, sketches on the street, to fully fledged gospel musical productions, such as Jimmy and Carol Owens' *The Witness*. Throughout the Bible God uses visual aids to help get his point across to his people. From Isaiah's going naked, Hosea's marrying a harlot, to Jeremiah at the potter's house, God has done everything in his power to illustrate his message, and help us *see* the gospel more clearly. We need to keep in mind that the gospel can be *seen* as well as heard (Rom. 15:21) and Jesus' parables were only pictures he drew in the minds of his hearers, to help them understand the kingdom of God a little more clearly.

Youth With A Mission's allegorical dramas, *Toymaker and Son* and *Tribute*, have been used to reach many thousands around the world. Trained teams have performed them everywhere from back alleys, prisons, to official receptions, and in nearly every nation on earth. Others, such as Mike Warnke and Isaac Air Freight, have used comedy as a way of presenting the truth of the gospel message, while André Cole uses *Gospel Magic* as an "interest door" to present the gospel to young people.

By its very nature, the potential of creativity is almost endless, and in the place of prayer we must allow the Holy Spirit to flood our minds and imaginations with ideas to use in effectively presenting the gospel.

The methods of evangelism discussed in this chapter are not just for the so-called "evangelists" in the church. They are for all Christians to be involved in, each doing his part as a worker in God's harvest field.

Chapter 6

Workers for the harvest

"This is what the kingdom of God is like. A man scatters seed on the ground. Night and day, whether he sleeps or gets up, the seed sprouts and grows, though he does not know how. All by itself the soil produces corn – first the stalk, then the ear, then the full grain in the ear. As soon as the grain is ripe, he puts the sickle to it, because the harvest has come." (Mark 4:26–9)

Several years ago I led a young man, Randy, to the Lord, and brought him home to live in our community and be discipled. For more than a month we poured ourselves into him, teaching him the Bible and the ways of God, and it seemed he was making good progress. Then, one morning we awoke to find that Randy had left and, in the process, stolen our complete sound system!

I was discouraged greatly by Randy's departure, and although he was not the first of our converts to backslide, he was the one who most surprised us. I began to feel that I was somehow responsible for Randy's lapse in faith, and was soon discouraged and wanting to give up. It seemed so much of my labour had been in vain.

In the midst of this turmoil, as I poured my heart out to God one day, I heard the voice of the Spirit whisper to my heart, "Danny, do you take the credit when you are able to lead someone to me?" "No Lord, you get all the glory from that," I quickly responded. "Then, do not take the blame when they backslide or reject the gospel," was the Lord's reply.

After this I discovered the above parable from Mark's gospel and began to meditate on it. Soon I began to feel a tremendous burden lift off my shoulders. I still felt bad about Randy's backsliding, and continued to pray for his restoration, but I no longer blamed myself for what had happened. I had done everything I could possibly do to see him firmly grounded in the gospel, and he had chosen to reject it, It was not God's fault, it was not my fault – it was Randy's choice.

It is not my job to save people, and neither can I keep them saved. I learned from the seed-planter parable that, in the harvest field, there is certain work that I must do, and there is other work that only God can do. My responsibility is to plough, plant, water and harvest the fruit when it is ripe. It is God's responsibility to ensure that the seed grows.

In the parable, the man planted the seed and then went to bed. However, while he slept the seed grew and, we are told, he did not know how this occurred (verse 27). The reason for this was because he could not personally cause the seed to grow, it was *beyond his control*. Only God can do that, it is his work. Jesus said, "No one can come to me unless the Father who sent me draws him" (John 6:44). It is the Father who causes the seed to grow, until it becomes "full grain" and ready for harvest. The same principle is given in Paul's letter to the Corinthians: "I planted the seed, Apollos watered it, but God made it grow. So neither he who plants nor he who waters is anything, but God only who makes things grow. For we are God's fellow workers . . ." (1 Cor. 3:6–9).

CONVERSION – A PROCESS

In the parable of the sower, Jesus teaches us about the process a person goes through in coming to him for salvation. The sickle harvesting the fruit represents a person being converted to Christ, while the seed being planted, and growing to the blade, ear, and full grain stages represents the spiritual growth a person goes through, even before salvation.

Seed in Jesus' parables most often refers to the Word of God, so the full grain in the ear represents that Word doing its complete regenerating work. Jesus spoke of this as being born again. After conception there is still nine months of "gestational" growth before the baby is actually born and, if it is removed earlier than this, it is unlikely to survive. Likewise, if corn is harvested too early, then the fruit will not be mature or long-lasting.

In both these illustrations we see the salvation experience as a process that takes time, gestation. There are some conversions that happen instantly, but in the vast majority of cases people come to the Lord over a period of time. During this time, the Lord of the Harvest uses a variety of different workers and situations to deal with a person's heart and draw him to himself. Few Christians would tell you they were converted the very first time they heard the gospel – it took time.

PRAY FOR WORKERS

Knowing the inner dynamics of conversion, and the time it takes for a person to come to salvation, Jesus exhorted us to pray for labourers that could be sent into the harvest field (Matt. 9:37–8; Luke 10:2). He did not ask us to pray for harvesters, sowers, ploughmen, or waterers exclusively, but for workers, someone who is willing to do whatever is needed to bring the seed to harvest.

I believe every unbeliever in the world today is at a particular stage of growth in their relationship to God. Perhaps they have heard the Word, but would not allow this seed to take root and grow in their life. Perhaps they heard and believed, but not enough to repent and commit their life to Christ (the blade). Possibly they are on the verge of salvation and just need a little more watering (the ear), or are ripe and ready to be harvested (full grain in the ear). This is not intended to be taken too literally, since not all unbelievers go exactly through all four stages of growth. It illustrates, though, the fact that we must allow room for the Word of God to mature in a person's heart *before* they are harvested.

Our task, as workers in God's harvest field, is to discern the point of spiritual growth a person is at, and what work needs to be done to bring them to the mature state, ready for harvesting. In our evangelistic mission we must see ourselves as workers with different pieces of equipment clipped to our spiritual belts, ready to use as the need arises. Perhaps, for instance, an unbeliever is hard-hearted and refuses to listen to the gospel. I might just try to love him and be his friend, letting my light shine by doing something good for him, and, using the hand trowel on my belt, break up the hard ground of his heart. Having broken up the ground, I can then pray that the Lord of the Harvest will send another worker who can nurture what has been begun in the unbeliever's heart (Matt. 9:37–8; Luke 10:2). If, on the other hand, a person has never heard the gospel and is willing to listen, I reach to the other side of my belt and pull some seed from my seed-bag. With it I sow God's word in that person's heart. If a person has been witnessed to and I sense all he needs is encouragement to come to salvation, I may unclip my watering can and water the seed that has already been sown. Perhaps the person is ripe and mature, and ready for harvesting, then I get out my sickle and harvest, leading them in a prayer of commitment to Jesus. While I always try to bring the people I meet to salvation, I have to continually remind myself that it is God who gives the increase, and that often takes time, depending on the level of growth an unbeliever is at.

There is no greater joy than seeing the seed we plant in a person's life grow and be harvested. Hitch-hiking home one day after a time of street witnessing I was picked up by a guy named Gene. I had forgotten about it, until ten years later when I met Gene in a department store. As we talked, he was happy to report to me that he, his wife, and family had recently received Christ and been baptised. He went on to thank me for the Bible I had given him as I climbed out of his car. It had planted the seed in his life, and he and his wife were still reading it. God had given the increase.

Back in my home town recently, I passed a young man on the street who looked familiar to me, so I stopped and asked him if he knew where it was we had met. At first he could not recall, then suddenly he said, "Now I remember. Five years ago I was a tramp living under a local bridge. One day you saw me sitting on the street with my backpack, approached me, and gave me a little red gospel booklet which told about Jesus. I used to read that little booklet every day you know." He hesitated for a moment and then continued, "Within six months of that I had been born again, and am now involved with a Catholic Charismatic church." This young man went on to thank me for the seed I had planted in his heart.

I have talked to hundreds of Christians about their conversion experience and found that in nearly every case, there was a time factor involved from the time they first heard the gospel till their conversion. In some cases this time factor ranged from just a few hours to forty years or more. Why some people take much longer than others on their route to salvation remains a mystery, but there are several factors to consider. First, there is tremendous spiritual warfare that goes on around a person's salvation. The Bible tells us that all unbelievers are blinded to the truth by the "god of this age" (2 Cor. 4:4). It often takes time to preach and pray these blinkers off a person's spiritual eyes so that they can see the "light of the knowledge of the glory of God in the face of Christ" (2 Cor. 4:6).

Secondly, even after the blinkers have been removed, the unbeliever still has a free will, and can choose to resist and reject the gospel, or open up and accept it. If they reject the gospel, then we need to pray and ask God to deal more severely with them. God will not force a person into salvation against his will, but he will put the pressure on! Saul of Tarsus, for example, was knocked to the ground, heard the audible voice of Jesus from heaven and was blinded for three days, before he was healed and filled with the Holy Spirit. God did not exactly force Saul's will, but made him an offer that was hard to refuse (Acts 9). God has his way of getting the attention of a selfish heart set on doing its own thing, and intercession becomes an important part of evangelism, since it releases the hand of God to deal in a person's life.

Other considerations in relation to the time factor of salvation are the degree of the power of God upon us as we witness, our unity in the church, and our example as believers to an unbelieving world.

When sharing the gospel we must never forget that GOD WANTS A PERSON TO BE SAVED MORE THAN WE DO. We must not think for a moment that he is not willing or able to save anyone and everyone. The Bible declares that God "wants all men to be saved and come to a knowledge of the truth" (1 Tim. 2:4); "The Lord is [. . .] not wanting anyone to perish but everyone to come to repentance" (2 Peter 3:9); "As surely as I live, declares the Sovereign Lord, I take no pleasure in the death of the wicked, but rather that they turn from their ways and live. Turn! Turn from your evil ways! Why will you die . . . ?" (Ezek. 33:11); "Whoever wishes, let him take the free gift of the water of life" (Rev. 22:17); "Whoever believes in him shall not perish but have eternal life" (Jn. 3:16). God is even now doing all he can to draw people to himself, and when we pray for the lost, or witness to a person, we are not twisting God's arm into saving them, but are co-operating with him in his effort to gather the harvest to himself.

WORKERS WORKING TOGETHER

"Do you not say 'four months more and then the harvest'? I tell you, open your eyes and look at the fields! They are ripe for harvest. Even now the reaper draws his wages, even now he harvests the crop for eternal life, so that the sower and the reaper may be glad together. Thus the saying, 'One sows and another reaps' is true. I sent you to reap what you have not worked for. Others have done the hard work and you have reaped the benefit of their labour" (John 4:35–8).

These verses show us tht evangelism is work, which is why Jesus asked us to pray for workers for the harvest. While it is God's work, he has chosen not to do it all by himself, and has called us to be co-labourers with him (1 Cor. 3:9; 2 Cor. 6:1; Mark 16:20). Regarding this work of evangelism, someone has said, "Without God, man cannot. Without man, God will not." So, the work of evangelism is a co-operative venture; we must be sure we do our part in close co-operation with God, in much the same way that Jesus was intimately united with the Father and did only what he saw the Father doing (John 5:19).

Co-operation is not only important between ourselves and God, but also between our fellow workers. Unity, after all, is to be the visual sign for the world to believe the gospel (John 17:21–3) and, according to Psalm 133, God commands a blessing, "even life for evermore" when believers are in unity with one another. The blessing of life for evermore is for the lost, not Christians, since we already have that blessing. However, that blessing will only be bestowed when we flow together in unity.

We see in Acts that when the believers in the early church were in "one accord" the Lord added to their number daily, "those who were being saved" (Acts 2:44–7). Later, after some internal disunity was taken care of, "The number of disciples in Jerusalem increased rapidly" and "a large number of priests became obedient to the faith" (Acts 6:7). In evangelism, God measures our effectiveness both corporately and individually. We are not a collection of Christians, but a many-membered body united to bring glory and honour to our Head, and as ". . . each member belongs to all the others" should live and work accordingly (Rom. 12:5).

Seeing this picture of the Lord of the Harvest directing workers who are patiently waiting for his command has totally changed my concept of witnessing and evangelism. Now, whenever I have the opportunity to witness to someone, I know I have been sent to that person by the Lord to either break up the ground, plant seed, water, or reap the harvest. Before going out in evangelism I now ask the Lord to lead me to those he has prepared so that I can do the required work and see the person brought closer to salvation. If I talk to someone and they receive Christ then I try to follow up on them, or arrange for another worker to do so. If the person does not receive Christ, I ask the Lord of the Harvest to send along another worker to take up where I left off. In this way God co-ordinates the efforts of his workers in all parts of the harvest field, responding to prayer, and sending those who have made themselves available as his workers wherever he sees there is work that needs to be done.

Mark, a twenty-three-year-old Californian, had been involved in drugs and found only emptiness, so had turned to Zen Buddhism. After eight months of Zen disciplines at a retreat centre in the Sierra mountains, he abandoned the mystic route and hitch-hiked south to

warmer weather. Near Santa Cruz he was picked up by a
Bible college student, John, who proceeded to share the
gospel with him. Mark listened but was still heavily
influenced by the teachings of Eastern mysticism, especially reincarnation, and informed John that it was
taught in the Bible. John, however, was ready with an
answer (1 Peter 3:15) and spent the next two hours with
Mark, talking and answering his questions, and showing
him from the Bible that it teaches not reincarnation, but
resurrection. John broke up the ground of Mark's heart
and planted the seeds of the gospel there. After dropping
him off, he prayed that the Holy Spirit would convict him
of sin (John 16:8) and lead other workers to water what
had been planted in Mark's heart.

One morning soon afterwards, as I prayed, I felt the
Lord impressing on me that I should go witnessing in the
town. By "divine appointment" I came across Mark,
handed him a tract, and began sharing with him about
Jesus. After about fifteen minutes of conversation we
departed, but before he left I gave him the address and
phone number of my church and invited him to come
along. I prayed that night, as I always do after having had
the opportunity to witness, that God would give increase
to the work I had done that day, and that more workers
would be sent into the harvest field (1 Cor. 3:6; Luke
10:2).

Walking along a beach several days later, Mark struck
up a conversation with Scott, a Christian who was
praying and reading the Bible. After a brief introduction,
Scott began to question Mark about his relationship
with the Lord. Mark admitted that he did not have a
relationship with God, but had been seriously thinking
about it lately. Scott realised that Mark was not ready for
harvesting quite yet, and so did not lead him in a prayer
of commitment, but instead gave him the address of his
church (which was the same as mine) and invited him to
attend. A few weeks later Mark did come to church,
heard the gospel again, and went forward to the altar to

give his life to Christ. From there he moved into our community "The Land", and was discipled. Today he is a Bible teacher being trained for missionary service.

In this example, the workers the Lord used were sensitive to the needs of the particular person they were dealing with. John did not have a self-righteous attitude to Mark's belief in reincarnation, and took the time patiently to show him the truth. The other workers, also, were not "sickle happy" and ready to cut the first signs of growth, but were sensitive to God's timing and the needs he wanted them to address in Mark's life. The result of this patient sensitivity to the Spirit was the lasting salvation of Mark.

SPIRITUAL ABORTIONS

After preaching at an open-air meeting on Union Square in San Francisco, a woman approached me and introduced me to her non-Christian friend from Germany who was interested in the message I had preached. She asked me many questions about Christianity and I patiently answered them and discussed the gospel with her, all the while trying to sense her need. In the midst of our conversation her friend interrupted with, "Do not worry about all your doubts, just ask Christ into your heart and the feelings will follow." That woman had made the same mistake many of us make when we imagine that a prayer of commitment is a cure-all for the woes of the unbeliever – if only they will accept Jesus then all will be well! However, we must not forget that it is essential for a person to believe before they are persuaded to receive. We must be patient with non-believers and not hurry them into something they are not ready to receive.

Paul told Timothy that "The Lord's servant must be

. . . kind to everyone, able to teach, not resentful. Those who oppose him he must gently instruct, in the hope that God will grant them repentance leading them to a knowledge of the truth, and that they will come to their senses and escape from the trap of the devil, who has taken them captive to do his will" (2 Tim. 2:24–6). This scripture shows us four agents involved in conversion; 1) the Christian witness (Rom. 10:14); 2) the non-Christian with a free will (Rom. 10:13); 3) the truth of the gospel (Rom. 10:17) and 4) God (John 6:44; Matt. 16:17). The non-Christian is under the snare of the devil, so we must be aggressive with our work in the harvest field, but this sometimes involves waiting patiently while God deals with someone he is drawing to himself. "See how the farmer waits for the land to yield its variable crop and how patient he is for the autumn and spring rains" (James 5:7).

When dealing with people I am seeking to win to the Lord I have not always exercised patience. For example, shortly after I had received the Lord I moved out of the house where I had been living, realising that the atmosphere of sex, drugs and rock and roll was not conducive to my spiritual growth. I left that house with a burden to see my old surfer friends, and in particular my closest friend Dave, won to the Lord. Being such a young Christian, I was high on zeal and low on wisdom. I would drive over to my previous house to share the gospel, but would always end up feverishly pressing Dave to make a decision for Christ. I would use fear, bribery, manipulation, and all the power I had. I thought it had all worked as I drove Dave to the ocean to baptise him. On the way there I explained about the rapture, the mark of the beast, and the antichrist that would soon arise, all of which I hoped would reassure him in what he was doing. But, as we walked out into the ocean, Dave told me he was not sure he was ready to go through with it. I assured him he was, as I dunked him under the water in the name of the Father, Son and Holy Spirit. I told him that since he had prayed the prayer of commitment the feelings would soon follow.

It did not take long for me to realise that I had not really led Dave to the Lord. All I had actually done was to get a sinner wet! I had manipulated Dave into saying a prayer that he did not really mean in his heart. He did not believe the gospel, he had not repented of his sins, and he surely did not want to follow Jesus. Proverbs tells us, "He who answers before listening – that is his folly and his shame" (Prov. 18:13). Dave had answered before he had really heard, because I was not patient enough to allow God to draw him to himself. In fact, my interference actually slowed down the Lord's dealings with Dave, to the point where I had to go back later and re-plant the seed in his heart, seed that would eventually bear fruit. Jesus promised that all those who reap *while the harvest is ripe*, will "harvest the crop for eternal life" (John 4:36). Several years later Dave did give his life to the Lord in a sincere and lasting way, and today is still one of my close friends, as well as a growing disciple.

There are in essence two types of people in the harvest field: those which Charles Finney categorises as "careless sinners", content with the present state of their life, and happy in unbelief and spiritual darkness, and those who are "seekers", who are spiritually hungry and diligently searching for truth. These are the people who, if not challenged with the gospel, often end up in religious cults or some other cause that offers to satisfy their hunger for truth. We need to be sure that we are challenging both categories of people with the gospel.

Jesus illustrated these two types of people in his parable about the man who found a treasure in a field, and the parable of the pearl merchant (Matt. 13:44–6). The pearl merchant could be described as a seeker, "looking for fine pearls", while the man who found the treasure in the field is like the careless sinner who, after stumbling upon treasure hidden in a field, went and sold all he had to buy the field. Mark, mentioned earlier, could be

categorised as a religious seeker, but we must not lose
hope for those who presently are not seeking at all.

Several years ago Phil and Rebecca, a young couple
who lived together, drove their pick-up truck down to
Santa Cruz. There Dawn, an old high-school friend of
Rebecca's, had arranged for the three of them to get
together. Dawn had recently become a Christian and was
anxious to share her new faith with them. However, after
several minutes of her witnessing, Phil told her in no
uncertain terms that he did not want to hear any more on
the subject. Dawn was sensitive to this, and for the next
couple of weeks just prayed for them, befriended them,
and spent time with them practising "light-shining"
evangelism.

One day she took them to a local beach, where some
young people happened to be playing slow-motion football. Inquisitively, Phil walked over to ask what they
were doing, and one of the players, a clean-cut eighteen-
year-old college student, told him they were part of a
summer outreach team and were using the football game
as a tool to share the good news of Jesus Christ. He asked
Phil if he knew the basic spiritual laws, and Phil admitted
he did not, so they spent time discussing them together.
Their conversation was fairly broad ranging, from
spiritual laws to modern events and the current world
situation ("interest doors"), and as they parted company
the student gave Phil a copy of an evangelistic book. Phil
accepted it readily and took it home to read.

Dawn meanwhile was continuing her visits, and one
day took them to an elderly Christian lady's home for
apple pie and ice cream. Margaret, the elderly lady, told
them how good it was to be saved, and shared her
testimony with them while serving the pie. She also
invited them to "The Land", our community, for dinner
that night, at which point I had the privilege of leading
them both to Jesus. Today they are strong Christians and
involved in the ministry. These two fitted our second
category of people; they were not seeking spiritual truth,

yet through many different people's diligent witness they were brought to salvation.

WHO IS THE CONVERT WINNER?

In Phil and Rebecca's testimony we see the parable of the seed-planter illustrated. The ground of their heart was hard, but Dawn ploughed it up and softened it with love, friendship and intercession. The Lord of the Harvest then went on to use the student on the beach, a Christian book, the loving testimony of an elderly saint, and even a physical place, "The Land", as tools to draw Phil and Rebecca to himself.

However, the above illustration raises an important point – which one of us actually led them to Christ? As the one who had led them in the sinner's prayer of commitment to Jesus, was I entitled to two notches on my Bible cover? Actually, the Bible tells us that it was the Father who led them to Jesus (John 6:65). It is the Father who reveals to the unbeliever who Jesus is (Matt. 16:17) and it is the Spirit who convicts of sin (John 16:8). If we would only realise that God is the soul winner, and that we are only helping him carry out his work, then we would see much fewer men revelling in the glory that should be God's alone. We must be careful that our evangelistic activities are not looked upon as spiritual scoreboard-keeping on how many souls each person has won to the Lord.

We must never take the credit for the fruit of the harvest field, and every time we have the privilege of helping someone come to the Lord, whether by ploughing, sowing, watering, or reaping, we should fall on our face in praise and exclaim, "To *God* be the glory, great things *He* has done!" We must make sure that God gets every bit of the praise for the fruit of evangelism:

"But 'Let him who boasts boast in the Lord'" (2 Cor. 10:17).

"The harvest is plentiful, but the workers are few. Ask the Lord of the harvest, therefore, to send out workers into his harvest field" (Luke 10:2; Matt. 9:37–8). We are called to be workers in God's harvest, which is riper today than it has ever been. From around the nations of the world reports continue to come in about the unprecedented receptivity of people to the gospel. From Jesus' teaching on evangelistic farming we can deduce that there would be an even greater harvest gathered into the kingdom of God, if he had more workers to work with him. Jesus' broken-hearted cry goes out today with more urgency than when he first uttered it two thousand years ago – will you be a worker?

Chapter 7

Decisions or disciples

"Therefore go and make disciples of all nations, baptising them in the name of the Father, and of the Son, and of the Holy Spirit, and teaching them to obey everything I have commanded you. And surely I am with you always, to the very end of the age" (Matt. 28:19–20).

When I first heard God's call to be involved in evangelism, I would sit back and have pipe-dreams about how God was going to use me to evangelise the world. With an inflated ego and selfish desire, I could see myself giving the altar call in a huge stadium, calling the crowds to come forward and accept Christ. I was "God's man of faith and power for the hour", "Come to Christ, hundreds of you, from all over the stadium, come forward, the buses will wait!" Indeed, in my early days that was my highest ideal for effective evangelism, if we could get enough evangelists to hold enough large rallies, have enough television and radio exposure, and distribute huge quantities of literature, then surely we would see the world evangelised in just a short time. However, as my experience in evangelistic work, and knowledge of the Word of God have grown, I can see that my early perspective on evangelism was both impractical and short-sighted. While some sorts of mass evangelism are needed, and are crucial to God's plan, they are not the only, or best, way of evangelising the world.

In the New Testament, evangelism and discipleship are closely linked, but they are not synonymous. A report by the American Institute of Church Growth indicated that at a 1976 Billy Graham crusade only 15 per cent of those converted actually ended up as active church members one year after the crusade (*Time Magazine*, 23 Jan 1978). This statistic is not quoted as a criticism of Billy Graham or mass evangelism. We acknowledge that his ministry has changed thousands of lives. Indeed, we should be praising God that the cup is 15 per cent full, rather than complaining that it is 85 per cent empty. The statistic, though, highlights an inherent weakness in mass evangelism – the evangelist cannot personally disciple all his converts. He does not have enough time to physically sit down and listen as each individual pours out their hurts and needs, and then see them established in a local church. He does not have the time to be a Paul to a young Timothy. His job as an evangelist is to proclaim the gospel and call unbelievers to repentance and faith. We need mass evangelism, and every other type of evangelism, so that we can use "all means" (1 Cor. 9:22). However, at the end of an evangelistic crusade, personal workers must take the time to do the discipling. I believe one of our great needs at present is for individual Christians who will help others come to faith in Christ and then lead them on to spiritual maturity. We, who are disciples ourselves, must also be disciple makers.

Billy Graham himself is quoted as saying, "The most important phase in an evangelistic campaign is the follow-up." This is because the object of the Great Commission is not merely to make converts, but rather to see these converts become mature disciples and faithful members of a local church. We can see from the way Jesus trained his disciples, and the strategy Paul had for church planting, that God is not satisfied with seeing people merely converted to him. He wants these converts to grow into spiritually mature disciples. Jesus commanded us to go and make disciples, not to obtain decisions.

As a new Christian, I had no idea of the biblical relationship between evangelism and discipleship, and would go out on the streets witnessing, buttonhole someone and press them to pray a prayer of commitment. When I achieved this objective I would proudly go home and chalk up another soul for the kingdom. It was not long before I had to re-examine both my methods and theology of evangelism, in the light of the little lasting fruit I saw among my "converts". In fact, many of the people I had "led to the Lord" still loved their sin, had no love for God, no desire to study the Bible and pray, and often did not even want to talk to me again! I began to see that there was a great weakness in my understanding of evangelism and its ensuing results.

Jesus said, "I chose you and appointed you to go and bear fruit – fruit that will last" (John 15:16). This verse came as a revelation to me. Through it I learned that God was not impressed with my glowing statistics on how many decisions I had recorded. God was interested in lasting fruit in my evangelism. He wanted to see disciples made, not just decisions recorded. My shotgun soul-winning may have been impressing my envious friends but, as far as God was concerned, my results were not causing rejoicing in heaven!

WORLD EVANGELISM – ONE AT A TIME

As part of my responsibilities as leader of a missionary-sending base I study many statistics on unreached groups, and seek God for ways to reach them. To be honest, it is sometimes discouraging to realise that there are not just millions, but billions of people on earth now who have never heard the gospel at all. Then there are the millions who have heard it and rejected it, and now need to hear it again.

Most of us have grown up in the instant generation, and are very much accustomed to having almost anything we desire within just a few moments. From McDonald's hamburgers to power tools and word processors, we have learned that anything we want is within easy reach. Unfortunately our instant mentality has crept into our view of evangelism, so that those of us from the western world have a tendency to set unobtainable goals in our pursuit of souls. When these are not achieved we are left feeling discouraged.

Once, in a prayer meeting, we were praying for fruit in individual evangelistic endeavours. With characteristic western zeal, one of the girls in the meeting exclaimed, "I claim a million souls to Christ – this year!" I said a sheepish amen to this request and thought to myself, "If you've got the faith – go for it!" She did not win her million souls to the Lord, and I have yet to speak in a soccer stadium, but does that mean neither of us are successful in evangelism? Should we feel discouraged and ineffective? After all, what really is successful evangelism?

I think if we had been Jesus we would have been very discouraged as we saw the crowds 'harassed and helpless, like sheep without a shepherd" (Matt. 9:36). But Jesus was not discouraged. He had a plan, a deliberate strategy he was going to implement during his three and a half years of ministry on earth. He knew that the most effective way to minister to the multitudes was through multiplication – multiplication of himself in his disciples, so that they in turn could minister to the crowds. Throughout scripture, we see Jesus calling his disciples aside to instruct them in his ways. This strategy at first seemed long and arduous, but its results would be long-lasting. Jesus avoided the obvious temptation to try and reach the multitudes all at once, knowing that if he took the time to pour himself into the twelve and disciple them, they in turn could go and disciple the multitudes.

In his book *The Master Plan of Evangelism*, Robert Coleman points out that in the course of Jesus' three and a half year ministry he spent increasingly more time training the twelve, and increasingly less time ministering to the multitudes. While not totally neglecting the masses, he was far more concerned with his long-range objective – making disciples of all nations – than he was with any short-cut that in the end would actually prolong reaching his goal. To quote Coleman:

> You cannot outwit the powers of darkness without strict adherence to Him who alone knows the strategy for victory [. . .] Only the Master's plan will work [. . .] This is a question that should be posed continually in relation to the evangelistic activities in the church. Are our efforts to keep things going fulfilling the Great Commission of Christ? Do we see an ever-expanding company of dedicated men reaching the world with the gospel as a result of our ministry? That we are busy in the church trying to work one program after another cannot be denied. But, are we accomplishing our objectives? (Robert Coleman, *The Master Plan of Evangelism*, p. 11.)

THE TIMOTHY PRINCIPLE

"And the things you have heard me say in the presence of many witnesses entrust to reliable men, who will also be qualified to teach others" (2 Tim. 2:2).

Paul's challenge to Timothy is to gather faithful disciples who can learn from him, and in turn can train other faithful disciples. The key word in this process is "faithful", not talented, rich, charismatic, or good-looking. "Like a bad tooth or a lame foot is reliance on the unfaithful in times of trouble." (Prov. 25:19). I have had both broken teeth and sprained ankles and know for a fact that you cannot put confidence in either. God wants faithful disciples who will stick to his strategy for victory,

even in times of trouble, who will seek out other faithful
disciples who want to grow and pour themselves into
them until they can disciple others. God wants those who
are willing to win, train, and send out others to do
likewise, for the cause of world evangelism.

How do we go about making a disciple? In Matthew
chapter 28, Jesus gives us the answer, "Go [. . .] baptising [. . .] teaching them to obey everything I have commanded you" (Matt. 28:19–20). First we must *go* to the
person, then we must seek to lead them to faith in Christ
and seal it with baptism. There then follows what is
sometimes a long and painstaking process where the
new believer is taught to follow and obey Jesus in every
area of life. We must be prepared for this to take time, as
we answer their questions, teach them the scriptures,
and help establish them in a local church. We must
become the new disciple's friend and be willing to spend
time just being with them, "Jesus ordained twelve. [. . .]
that they might be with him" (Mark 3:14).

In disciple making Jesus told us to teach them to obey
all his commands, and that includes his last com-
mandment – to go and make disciples – disciple-making
disciples!

An important advantage in the Timothy principle for
the multiplication of disciples is that most Christians are
not mass evangelists and would feel uncomfortable
ministering to large crowds. They may not be able to
believe God for hundreds to come forward at a crusade,
but they can believe for one they can take and disciple. I
challenge you to ask God today for a Timothy. Win him,
train him, and send him back to the world to do for
someone else what you have done for him.

A simple comparison of multiplication and addition
reveals the wisdom of the Timothy principle. Imagine,
for example, an evangelist winning one thousand people
to Christ every day, working 365 days a year with no time
off. In thirty years of ministry he will have added over ten
million people to the Kingdom of God. Now, imagine a

Christian like you, who is capable of winning one person a year to Christ. You spend your year discipling this lone convert to the point where he can go and disciple another, and then he spends his next year winning and discipling another. In the meantime you are also discipling another, and so the process goes on. If this were to go on unbroken, in only twenty-five years sixteen million people would have been won to Christ, and all because of your initial willingness and involvement. We can see that if the world is going to be evangelised then we must use principles of multiplication, and not just addition.

Several years ago I took a team of twenty-three Discipleship Training School students from Youth With A Mission to Fiji for a three-month outreach. During the first half of the outreach we were involved in a lot of door-to-door evangelism and street witnessing, as well as ministry in local churches, and a Thursday night new believers' Bible study. On Saturdays we held an open-air meeting in the town centre, which was reaping good results. Things were going well until the immigration department informed us we could no longer continue to do what we were doing on tourist visas. They told us that we could do no more ministry whatsoever, not even sing a song in a church.

We were all very discouraged by this and began to seek the Lord for a new strategy. God soon showed us that we must obey the ruling of the immigration department and stop all ministry. However, I challenged each student and staff member to ask God for two people they could win and disciple during the remainder of our time in Fiji. My thinking was, that if we could leave behind forty-six transformed Fijians then our outreach would have been fruitful.

Some of the team began following up on people they had led to the Lord during the first half of the outreach, while others discipled nominal Christians who had no grounding in their faith. Some went out as tourists and asked God to lead them to the right people, while still others began befriending their neighbours and reaching out to them. This was all accomplished without the ministry tools we were so used to – guitars, tracts, Bible studies, open-air meetings and the like.

In evaluating the success of this outreach several months later, I was delighted to find that two churches we had worked with had baptised thirty new members who were now attending regularly and growing in their relationship with God. There were other new disciples in several other churches, and many nominal Christians had been strengthened in their faith. God's principles of evangelism work, since he is the one who designed them and gave them to us in his Word.

The Timothy principle also spreads out the work load of evangelism. More people are able to be released to the work of evangelism, so the load of work is shared amongst a greater number of workers. There is also less chance of someone getting all the glory for the fruit produced.

Ephesians four teaches on the five-fold ministry of the Holy Spirit, and we find that apostles, prophets, evangelists, pastors, and teachers have all been given to the church to "prepare God's people for works of service" (Eph. 4:11–12). In other words, "professional" ministers are not called to the primary task of ministry, but are to prepare God's people, the average Christians, to undertake that task. *We need to see that we are all called to be God's ministers of reconciliation*, and in so doing are His ambassadors and priests. (2 Cor. 5:18–20; 1 Peter 2:5–9; Rev. 5:10). The work of discipling is for all of us to be involved in.

The day the revelation hit me that God could actually use me to bring someone to himself, is one I will never forget. I was in a worship meeting and looked across the aisle to see my friend Steve, hands raised in the air worshipping God. We first met when I picked him up and gave him a lift to where he was staying. I had known Steve as an unbeliever, and had also had the joy and privilege of seeing him come under conviction of sin and finally surrender his life to the Lord. As I reflected on it in church that day I realised that God could even use me, an unworthy servant, as an instrument in his hands. I began to weep with joy and thanksgiving. Leading a person to Christ is one of the greatest feelings a person can ever have in this life.

I think the only greater thrill in life is seeing someone you have led to the Lord lead someone else to the Lord in turn. As the bumper-sticker says, "Happiness is Being a Grandparent", and I can tell you my greatest feelings of joy in the Christian life have come as I have seen my spiritual children reproduce themselves. Imagine the joy it must have brought to Jesus as he looked down the corridors of time and prayed for his disciples and all those who would come to believe in him because of their testimony (John 17:20). Paul, too, must have been beside himself with joy when he learned of his spiritual offspring, the Thessalonians, that "The Lord's message rang out from you not only in Macedonia and Achaia – your faith in God has become known everywhere, therefore we do not need to say anything about it." (1 Thess. 1:8). John also told Gaius that he could have no greater joy than to hear that his spiritual children were walking in the truth (3 Jn. 4).

Realising the link between evangelism and disciple-ship, and that people need a place where they could grow into mature Christians, I began praying for a house similar to the Shekinah House in Santa Cruz, where I had been discipled. God, however, provided not one, but five houses on a piece of property right in the heart of town which we named "The Land", and a handful of us moved in.

As a young leader at "The Land" I went through my share of frustrations and changes. We faced every kind of trial imaginable, discouragement, set-backs, disappoint-ment, financial problems, lives being threatened, but through everything, including my spiritual immaturity,

God was able to use "The Land" to bring people to himself and see them discipled.

What a joy it is for me to recount some of the lives that were changed for the glory of God during this period. There is Danny, who had just arrived in town from New York when I met him. He had been in five different mental institutions by the time he was twenty-one, and while in New York had attempted suicide three times. He was gloriously saved and mentally healed, and is today a missionary in Japan.

Then there is Kevin, an ex-Moonie, who moved in with us at "The Land" after his conversion. Within several years he was a missionary in the Philippines, where he is an elder, and leader in Youth With A Mission.

Scott, who was saved and discipled by us, is now a missionary in Japan, while Larry, who used to grow marijuana in his garden, became a missionary to Nepal after he was converted and discipled at "The Land".

Frank was converted at a restaurant, and was discipled by us. He is now leading a Youth With A Mission School of Evangelism that trains and sends missionaries to Asia.

I mention these people, not to take any credit for myself, but to illustrate the necessity of discipleship. As we take the time to train and ground a new believer in the faith, they in turn can be released to go and make other disciples.

A LOOK AT WESLEY'S METHODS

John Wesley believed the world was his parish, and organised his converts into small groups where "the beginnings of faith in a man's heart could be incubated into saving faith in the warm Christian atmosphere of the society, rather than in the chill of the world" (J. Glenn Gould, *The Hurt of Man*). He understood implicitly the biblical connection between evangelism and discipleship, and put as much emphasis on discipleship as he did on evangelism. The result of this was one of the most powerful evangelistic and missionary movements in church history. It is said that he "would refuse to preach in any place where he could not follow it up by organised societies with adequate leadership" (Sydney C. Dimond, *The Psychology of the Methodist Revival*). Wesley's ministry is best summed up in these few short words, "He was out to make disciples – disciples who would renew the whole church" (Howard Snyder, *The Radical Wesley*).

BABY CARE

One of the most dangerous things I have observed in the body of Christ is the insensitive way we treat new Christians. Whenever a baby is born, he or she gets all the attention, as mummy, daddy, grandparents and friends all gather round to tickle, and enjoy this new life that has come into the world. In a similar way, I believe, this care and attention should also be extended to baby Christians who are born again. Just as a new baby explores his new environment, looking and crawling around, and getting into everything within reach, so spiritual babies need the liberty to do the same. Suddenly they are in a new environment, the biblical Christian culture, and are expected to be at Bible studies, prayer meetings, and the like, which may take them by surprise. We must be sensitive and realise that a baby Christian does not grow into a spiritual giant over night. It takes time, and we must allow them the liberty of that time.

Those of us who are older in our relationship with the Lord need especially to watch that we do not require more obedience from a new believer than God does. A mother, after all, will expect a lot less from her two-week-old infant than from her eight-year-old son. Sometimes, in our zeal to preach repentance, we add to God's commands and expect more faith from a baby Christian than they have the capacity for.

Statistics have shown that younger Christians are often the most effective evangelists, and there are several reasons for this. They still have a zeal and excitement about the Lord; they have not become so immersed in the Christian culture that they are alienated from the world, and so still have unsaved friends. But one of the main reasons for their effectiveness, is that they can understand and relate to both unbelievers and new Christians, since they themselves are often still spiritual toddlers.

When I was first converted out of the drug culture I earnestly believed my dog Joshua was going to go to heaven, and while I wanted to move into the Shekinah House for discipling, I refused to unless my dog could come with me. I desperately needed discipling, but my dog was a high priority in my "baby" mind. Fortunately the brothers leading the ministry loved me and were sensitive to my needs, so gave me some breathing room, allowing Joshua and me to move in. Looking back at it now I praise God for their understanding and tolerance.

Another friend of mine, Kerry, was selling ounce-bags of marijuana when he was saved. After his conversion he proceeded to add Gospel of John booklets as a bonus with what he was selling! Now that was a foolish thing to do! It was a baby thing to do! Someone was loving and kind with Kerry and showed him a more excellent way, so that he stopped selling drugs altogether.

Garry was also newly saved out of the drug culture, and was convicted by the Holy Spirit for selling marijuana. One day he gathered up all his marijuana and took it out to the beach where he made an altar and offered the drugs as a burnt offering to the Lord! From there Gary went on to become a strong Christian and effective evangelist, but he started out as a baby. Be gentle with babies!

Chapter 8

Your Kingdom come:

The missions mandate

"When you pray, say, Our Father in heaven, hallowed be your name, your kingdom come. May your will be done on earth as it is in heaven" (Luke 11:2).

In response to the disciples' question on how to pray, Jesus gave us what has come to be known as the Lord's Prayer. In this prayer, the very first petition we are instructed to place before the Father is that his kingdom will come and his will be done on earth as it is already being done in heaven. If it is God's will for his Kingdom to come on earth, then what on earth is the kingdom of God? The answer to this question is crucial if we are to properly understand Christian missions.

From the beginning God has desired that mankind rule over all his creation, and, when he had finished his original handiwork in Adam and Eve, he blessed them and told them to "be fruitful and multiply and replenish the earth, and subdue it and have dominion [rule] over the fish of the seas, birds of the air, and over every living thing that moves upon the earth" (Gen. 1:28; see also Psalm 8:4–6; Heb. 2:6–8). Adam and Eve, through their fall, forfeited the right to rule on earth as God had intended. God, however, was not to be side-tracked from his original plan by this, since he had determined in his heart that his kingdom would come.

He then called a Babylonian named Abraham and

declared his intention to bless him and make him a blessing to all the peoples of the earth (Gen. 12:1–3). Through Abraham, God was going to raise up a nation that would represent his rule (or kingdom) to all the nations of the earth (see Exod. 19:5–6; Deut. 30:1; Num. 14:20; Psalms 67; 96; 98; Isa. 49:5–6; 66:18–19; Zech. 9:9–10). On several occasions God repeated this promise to Abraham, and then confirmed it with an oath, swearing by himself (Gen. 22:15–18; Heb. 6:13–19). Isaac and Jacob were also to receive this same promise that their offspring would be a blessing to all peoples of the earth (Gen. 26:4; 28:14).

Israel, for the most part, failed in its God-given mission, so God had to establish the Levitical priesthood. The nation chosen to be a kingdom of priests now needed priests (the Levites) themselves, because of their failure to obey God's plan. Eventually God's own Son would have to declare to the Jews that "the kingdom of God shall be taken from you and given to a people who will produce its fruit" (Matt. 21:43). That people he has now chosen is the Church (1 Peter 2:9) and the "fruit" is the obedience of Jew and Gentile to the king of the kingdom (see Matt. 3:8; Luke 3:8–9).

THE GOSPEL OF THE KINGDOM

The word kingdom in both the Old and New Testaments refers to the right to rule, or the authority exercised by a king. While scripture declares, "his kingdom rules over all"(Psalm 103:19), Satan has led captive, and out from under God's authority, a host of rebels. However, when Jesus returns he will establish, once and for all, God's kingdom in all its fullness, and every knee shall bow in submission to him, whether the knee-benders like it or not! (Phil. 2:11) Our job in the meantime is to preach the gospel of the kingdom (Matt. 24:14) and give people the opportunity to bow their knees willingly, before it is too late. We are to keep busy at his work until he comes (Luke 19:13).

The Great Commission to reach all nations was not just an afterthought Jesus had when he established the New Covenant. It has been the plan of God from the beginning, he has always wanted lovingly and righteously to rule all the peoples of the earth. Paul tells us that the gospel of grace and the gospel of the kingdom are one and the same when he says, "The scripture foresaw that God would justify the Gentiles by faith, and announced the gospel in advance to Abraham: 'All nations will be blessed through you'" (Gal. 3:8). The command to be a blessing to all peoples, and so to extend God's kingdom, given to Adam, then Abraham, Isaac and Jacob, is the very backbone of the Bible (see Acts 3:25; 13:47; Rom. 1:5; 16:26; Rev. 5:9; 7:9).

BLESSING, FRUITFULNESS AND MULTIPLICATION

We find that as God gave his "kingdom mandate" to Abraham, Isaac and Jacob, he also gave three promises of blessing, fruitfulness, and multiplication alongside it (Gen. 12:3; 17:6–20; 18:18; 22:17; 26:4; 26:24; 28:3). Today, as then, God wants to bless his people, but these blessings are not meant to be ends in themselves, but that we will be fruitful and multiply. God, who was blessed in himself, created man to share that great blessing, so that those of us who are "of faith are blessed along with Abraham" (Gal. 3:9). However, just as Abraham became a channel of blessing to all peoples of earth, so too must we.

Throughout history, God's people have had a tendency to hoard his blessings to themselves, not passing them on. Jesus gave specific instructions for the early disciples to carry the gospel to "Jerusalem, and in all Judea and Samaria and to the ends of the earth" (Acts 1:8). Despite this they stayed on in Jerusalem, even after fierce persecution had driven all other Christians out of the city to those places God had intended them to go (Acts 8:1–4). Apart from occasional short mission trips, the original apostles stayed on in Jerusalem, despite Jesus' instruction for them to go to the ends of the earth (see Don Richardson, *Eternity in Their Hearts*, p. 156). Perhaps this is why the Holy Spirit chose to focus most of the book of Acts on Paul, the apostle who obeyed God's command to be "a light for the Gentiles" (Acts 13:46–7).

Following on from Paul's example, Christians for the next two and a half centuries went everywhere and preached the gospel, eventually seeing the whole Roman Empire surrendering to it and embracing Christianity. Shortly after this, the church began to lose her missionary zeal and doctrinal purity, and entered the Dark Ages, where for the next thousand years the Great Commission was largely forgotten.

During the Reformation under Luther, Calvin and Zwingli the church was still not fully committed to its obligation of reaching the ends of the earth. This was due in part to Luther's belief that the second coming of Christ was so imminent that there was not time for world evangelism, and that the Great Commission was only binding on the original apostles. The doctrine of justification by faith for the most part remained locked up in Europe, and we are given no evidence that the Reformers actively sought to allow the gospel to be fruitful and multiply cross-culturally.

It was not until 1722 that the flame of world evangelism was rekindled, when Count Nicolas Zinzendorf established the Moravian missionary movement. Motivated by the slogan, "May the Lamb that was slain receive the just reward of his suffering", missionaries landed on all six continents within twenty years. Within one hundred and fifty years over two thousand Moravian missionaries, most of them young, had been sent overseas. Indeed, it was Moravian missionaries who led John Wesley to faith in Christ, and they also greatly influenced William Carey, who was to become known as the "father of modern missions".

Carey carried the torch lit by the Moravians, and in 1792 published his classic work, *An Enquiry into the Obligation of Christians to use Means for the Conversion of the Heathen"*. In 1793 Carey himself sailed for India, but his publication fuelled the fire of missions, and soon in England, Scotland, Holland, and America there was much interest in evangelism and missions. Where there had been little concern for the peoples in the vast regions of Asia, Africa, India and Latin America, now people were anxious to see the gospel shared with them.

With Hudson Taylor's pioneer work into China last century, another wave of missionaries was released to new frontiers of the globe. Over six thousand missionaries were served by Taylor's China Inland Mission, and his vision to reach into the interior of unreached nations became the impetus for scores of other missionary organisations. Since that time many others have followed the principles of Carey and Taylor and gone out to the ends of the earth to preach the gospel.

Because the foundations of world evangelism have been well laid, we can optimistically look from our vantage point in the 1980s and see all that is being done to further the gospel of the kingdom worldwide. While there are still areas of the world that lie in darkness, in many others the church is flourishing. For example, in Brazil about three thousand new churches are established each year, and in Africa and Asia one thousand new churches open their doors every Sunday. The church is growing so fast in Africa that at the present rate by the year 2000 nearly 50 per cent of its population south of the Sahara will be Christian, while in many parts of Latin America it grows three times faster than the population. The numbers of Protestants there has soared from fifty thousand in 1900 to well over twenty million in 1980. Asia also is experiencing unprecedented church growth, and in a country such as South Korea, where there were virtually no Christians at all one hundred years ago, today close to 30 per cent of the population is Christian. The same is true of Indonesia, Singapore, the Philippines and parts of India, where tremendous growth has also taken place in the last several years. In all, approximately 78,000 new Christians are added to the worldwide body of Christ daily (David Barret, *World Christian Encyclopedia*).

It is interesting to note, however, that Europe has replaced Africa as the dark continent, and is the only region on earth where Christianity is actually decreasing in numbers, as secularisation and liberal theology have joined hands to push back the gospel. The Muslim world, with its 800 million inhabitants (mostly in the Middle East, North Africa, India and Indonesia), is the most resistant region to the gospel. This is due in part to a lack of workers, since although this region constitutes nearly 25 per cent of the world's population, only one per cent of the North American missionary force is working there.

Along with the Muslim world, the other areas of greatest need for missionaries are; the Chinese (one billion), Hindus (600 million), Buddhists (250 million). The challenge before the church of the 1980s is still great, but it is a challenge that is surpassed only by the opportunity we presently have to spread the gospel to the ends of the earth. The opportunity is before each of us, and the promises of God are with us – Jesus said GO!

GET INVOLVED NOW!

There is no time to waste. Every day that we are indifferent to our responsibility to obey the Great Commission is a day lost to the cause of Christ. God wants us to see the world as he sees it, having a global perspective of his eternal purposes in Christ.

I first began to see God's perspective on the world several years ago on a trip to Disneyland with my family. We were on a ride called "It's a Small Small World", where little boats go through tunnels into imaginary countries. In these countries are dolls of all the different nationalities on earth, all singing with glee, as if they had no cares, "It's a small world after all." There they were, dolls from Holland, China, Arabia, America, Spain, Russia and Africa, all holding hands and smiling happily in their native costumes, and I suddenly began to weep. By the time we had reached the end of the ride I could hardly see through the tears in my eyes. When we came out into the light again my wife looked at me shocked and my son Daniel asked me what was wrong. I tried to express to them what I was feeling, "It's not a small world. It's not a happy world. It's a wicked, dirty, sinful world and for the most part it's being run by the devil, while people are singing their way to hell!" The people, of course, waiting to go on the small world ride looked at me as though I had gone crazy, and Daniel was not exactly sure what to make of his daddy either. I suddenly saw on that ride that the story-book image of the small world is exactly what Satan wants us to see so that he can keep us indifferent to the millions who perish without Christ. This is not to say that Disneyland is of the devil, but it certainly does not accurately portray reality as God sees it.

The fact is, there is a harvest that is ripe in a field where there are painfully too few workers: "Open your eyes and look at the fields. They are ripe for harvest" (Jn. 4:35).

We must become an army of World-Christians who are
not content just to be "normal". We are not normal, we
are "ecclesia" – the called-out ones. Called out from the
darkness of this world to light, so that we can rescue
those who are still perishing in darkness without Christ.
The normal Christian life is to be the radical Christian life,
as different from the lifestyle of this world as light is from
darkness. As we learned from Abraham's life, God has
blessed us so that we in turn will be a blessing to the
nations of the earth.

BURDEN, VISION AND WORK

The book of Nehemiah gives insight into three ways
we can become involved with God in his global cause.
Nehemiah hears of the awful plight of his brethren in
Jerusalem who have survived the captivity. The city wall
is broken down (symbolic of lack of protection from
enemies), the gates are burned (symbolic of burnt-out
evangelism), and the people are in distress. After hearing
this news, Nehemiah immediately sets himself to pray
and fast and seek God's face over the situation.

1. DEVELOPING THE BURDEN: Nehemiah did not have to
seek God for a burden, for he already had one, so his
fasting and praying was a natural reaction to hearing the
news that God's work was in trouble. He was *already*
close to God's heart, so when God was burdened he was
burdened. Indeed, holiness has been defined as hating
what God hates and loving what he loves, and, as a
branch takes root in the vine it begins to take on the
characteristics of the vine, one of which is a love of
righteousness and a hatred of evil.

By burden I mean having a concern for the things God
is concerned for, and not a negative attitude that leads to
legalism. After all Jesus said his burden was light (Matt.

11:30), but it was none the less a burden. Do you think God is concerned about the three thousand language groups who have no scriptures in their language as yet, or the 16,750 distinct ethnic groups who have no Christian witness among them? What about the nearly one billion starving and malnourished people in the world, and the millions of babies that are killed every year by abortion: does God care about them?

Yes, I believe God is vitally concerned about these situations, and wants us to share this concern (or burden) with him so that we, in turn will do something about it. There are two ways we can develop this burden for the world, the first is to pray and intercede on behalf of those who are in darkness. As we draw close to God in this way he is able to impart to us his heart for a situation. The second way to develop a burden is simply to get involved. Often people who are actively involved in reaching out to the lost are unaware of the weight of the burden they carry, since seeing needs and meeting them moves them in both prayer and action.

2. CATCH THE VISION: Someone has said, "A vision without a burden makes imagery; a burden without a vision makes drudgery; but a burden with a vision makes a missionary." Soon after Nehemiah had prayed and fasted about the situation in Jerusalem, God turned his burden into a vision. He began to see the rebuilt city wall, the gates re-hung, and the people in safety. In much the same way we must allow God to expand our vision for a situation so that we will be motivated to action.

God will never give us a burden for a situation unless he also intends to give the positive side of it – a vision to see the situation changed. Jesus, moved with a burden of compassion at facing a workerless but ripe harvest field, implanted a vision in his disciples to see themselves as workers for the harvest (Matt. 9:36–8). All major endeavours for God start first with a burden which later becomes a vision. For instance, William Booth's burden for the down-and-outs of London was turned into the

vision for the Salvation Army, and the heart Of Africa
Mission was started by C. T. Studd after he received a
burden for the tribes of darkest Africa. In the same way,
Teen Challenge was born out of David Wilkerson's burden for inner-city youth, while Loren Cunningham's
burden to see young people used in missions resulted in
the birth of Youth With A Mission.

What is your vision? Do you believe God can use you in
an active way in his global task of reaching the nations?
Perhaps you think you are not qualified. You are probably right! But then, neither was Jeremiah, "I do not
know how to speak. I am only a child" (Jer. 1:6). Nor was
Gideon's army qualified when just three hundred men
went to battle the Midianites who were "innumerable"
(Judges 6:5; 7:6). As Gideon's army came close to the
point where it would be cut to its final size, God instructed him to take the remaining ten thousand men
down to the water for their final test. Those who had their
own needs as top priority, the ones bowing down on
their knees to drink, their eyes fixed only on the water,
were sent home. Those who lapped the water out of their
hands while their eyes scanned the horizon for danger
were the ones God was interested in using to demonstrate his power. In his wisdom God chose only three
hundred men to fight the hordes of Midianites, but they
were three hundred men of faith and vision.

To catch the vision for world evangelism and the
multiplication of God's kingdom that can come through
us, we can learn a lesson from Gideon and his army.
They were not fearful, but trusted God and fixed their
eyes on him and his ability to defeat the enemy through
them. While we need to examine ourselves to see where
our heart really is in relation to God's work, we must also
avoid the pitfall of "onion peeling" introspection, where
the more we peel, the more it smells, and the more we
cry! (2 Cor. 13:5) Once we have examined ourselves then
we must fix our eyes on Jesus where, like Gideon's army,
our needs will be met.

3. DOING THE WORK: The book of Nehemiah ends happily with the work on the city wall being completed, a direct result of Nehemiah's obedience to the burden and vision God had given him. After God has given us a heart for, and perspective on, a particular situation he also expects us to be available to him so that he can work through us and fulfil his desire. This, after all, is the meaning of seeking the kingdom first.

Ultimately the work of evangelism can only be accomplished when each of us plays our own part in building up the body, and co-operating with others who are also playing their part. "The whole body joined and held together by every supporting ligament, grows and builds itself up in love, as each part does its work" (Eph. 4:16).

God has chosen to use many different parts, all working together to fulfil his purposes for world missions. Below are listed some practical ways in which you could become involved in the work of missions and take the gospel of Jesus to the nations of the world:

SHORT-TERM MISSIONS: My concept of a missionary had always been of a "square" who could not succeed in normal life, and so would bury himself in the jungles among the pygmies of Africa. Or, sometimes I thought they were someone like the bigot Abner Hale in Michener's *Hawaii* who sought to destroy the native culture.

My first missionary experience came on a Youth With A Mission short-term outreach to Fiji in the South Pacific. Here I worked alongside a group of people just like me, who were not "squares", or bigots, but were normal people committed to taking the gospel cross-culturally, in a sensitive way, to the people of Fiji. Once I had tasted world missions in this setting I was hooked for life.

Perhaps a short-term outreach, or "unholy land tour" is what you need to get a realistic picture of what missions is all about and what a missionary does. This experience can be valuable whether or not you feel God is calling you to the mission field. Organisations such as

Youth With A Mission, Operation Mobilisation, and others each year have various short-term programmes and special outreaches worldwide that you can be involved in. These programmes all provide exciting, "hands-on" missionary involvement, and may well whet your appetite for more!

Some groups, YWAM, OM, Last Days Ministries, and Horizon International, for example, offer short-term discipleship training opportunities that lead directly to missions involvement in just a few months. Perhaps you could consider this after school, before you get settled into college or a career.

MERCY MINISTRIES: Here, many groups offer both long- and short-term involvement in everything from food distribution, medical work and nutritional services, to building and providing shelter for people. War, natural disasters and famine in recent years have created a vast need for this sort of specialised work among the twenty million or more refugees scattered across the face of the globe. Many of these people have been stripped of everything except life itself, and Jesus said that if we serve the least of his brethren then we are in turn actually serving Him (Matt. 25:40).

BIBLE TRANSLATION: Of the 7010 distinct living languages in the world today, there is no Bible translation in over 3000 of them. Wycliffe Bible Translators and other groups provide practical linguistic training and help for those who desire to see God's Word translated and published among every "tribe and language and people and nation" (Rev. 5:9). Dedicated long-term workers are needed in this area to assist at all stages of the translation process.

THE SMALLER HALF OF THE WORLD: Today, over 50 per cent of the world's population is under eighteen years of age. Children require a specialised strategy of evangelism that is suited to their particular needs. Many evangelical missions have formed specialised branches of their ministries to minister to the needy and open area of child evangelism. Perhaps God is calling you to this ministry.

SUPPORT WORKERS: David told his people that those who stayed at home to look after the baggage would get the same rewards as those who were on the frontlines of the battle (1 Sam. 30:24). There are many missions that require several support workers for every missionary on the frontlines doing the direct work of evangelism. Administrators, secretaries, public relations people, accountants, kitchen workers, mechanics, construction workers, and maintenance people are all needed to keep the machinery of missions moving towards its objective. No matter what talents you have God can use them effectively in missions.

SUPPORT GIVERS: Missionaries are mostly supported in their endeavours by people like you and me who give voluntary contributions towards their work. In regard to this, one of the questions I am often asked is, "Why aren't missionaries today self-supported like Paul?" To this question there are several answers. Firstly, many countries do not issue work permits to foreigners, in order to preserve jobs for their own people. Secondly, the less concerned a missionary has to be with making money to pay his living costs, the more time he can spend involved in the work of the gospel, which, after all, is the only reason he is in the country. Then, thirdly, Paul was not always self-supported and gladly received financial aid from various churches (Phil. 4:14–18).

We need to make it our practice to give generously and regularly to missions, and one good way to do this is through giving directly to the worker in the field. Giving this way has the advantage that you know exactly where your money is going, while at the same time giving the feeling that you are personally involved in their ministry. This should be a two-way thing, however, and the person being supported needs to communicate regularly what he is doing to those who are supporting him.

Each year Americans give one billion dollars to

missions. While this sounds like a wonderful contribution, we need to consider that we spend nearly that amount yearly on chewing gum and seven times as much on pet food. Perhaps this will stir us to dig a little deeper in our pockets the next time we hear of a missionary who has a need.

CHURCH PLANTING: In light of the fact that Jesus commanded us to go and make disciples of all nations, we need to be establishing among the 16,000 groups who have no permanent Christian witness structures that will nurture and establish disciples in God's Word. Pioneer church planting is perhaps the most barren area of mission work today. Many young people are desperately needed to lay down their lives by going to an unreached area, learning the language and culture, evangelising, and eventually planting a church there. They also need to be committed to staying until strong local leaders are able to assume the responsibility of running the church and caring for the spiritual needs of the area. Establishing and multiplying churches, I believe, is the battlefield where world evangelism will be won or lost. So, we need to see an army of committed people in every area of the harvest field following Paul's methods – establishing churches that will multiply themselves, training up national leaders, and moving on to establish another church elsewhere (2 Cor. 10:16).

Ultimately church planting is the bottom line in world missions. After someone has been won to Christ they must have a structure into which they can fit and feel comfortable as they grow and reproduce themselves. All missionary work is a means to an end, that of making disciples, disciples who need nurturing and training. Short-term evangelistic teams and travelling evangelists should keep this in mind and endeavour to work closely with existing, lively churches in the area where they are working. If there are no churches that can mould strong disciples out of the converts made, then one needs to be established. Too many failures have taken place because well-meaning evangelists have lost sight of their long-term objectives. We must constantly be monitoring our results to see if we are really achieving what we set out to do.

I was converted during what is now known as the "Jesus Movement", and one of the characteristics I noticed about this movement was an unquenchable zeal for outreach by converted ex-drug addicts and hippies. There was a strong emphasis on both personal and mass evangelism in the form of street-witnessing and preaching, door-to-door evangelism, literature distribution, as well as gospel concerts, marches and rallies. As the movement developed on into the 1970s there was a swing towards discipleship, where there was emphasis on teaching, training and equipping the believers. We began hearing much about Christian community, church unity and relationships within the body, while the cassette-tape ministry began to boom as pastors were busy about the job of feeding their sheep.

In the 1980s I have noticed a swing back towards evangelism, but with a more mature emphasis. Most church leaders now agree that evangelism without follow up, and discipleship without an evangelistic thrust, are both faulty. Groups that have no vision of multiplying themselves are in danger of becoming mere Christian country clubs and catching the disease someone has termed "koinonitus" – an overdose of fellowship! Nature shows us that inbreeding within the same family will produce deformity, and the same is true in the spiritual realm.

I believe God has been laying the groundwork for a mighty thrust of the gospel that will reach to every corner of our world. We need the evangelistic fervour of the 1960s coupled with the call to commitment heard in the 1970s so that we will have mature, calculated strategies for reaching the world in the 1980s. God is raising up an army who, in these last days, will overcome the devil, "by the blood of the Lamb, and by the word of their

testimony they did not love their lives so much as to
shrink from death" (Rev. 12:11). He wants modern-day
William Careys and Hudson Taylors who will pioneer
frontier regions of the world for him. He wants disciples
that are not just engaged in theological controversy and
debate, who are not arguing about the timing of the
second coming but are out busily proclaiming the good
news of what Jesus did at his first coming. He wants an
army that will not be asking, "How much does it cost?"
But rather will be asking, "Where do I pay?" They will
not want to know how much sin they can get away with
and still be saved, but will be asking, "How much can I do
to further the kingdom?" He wants people who are
consumed with love for him, whose desires are one with
his, and who will not be content until the earth is "full of
the knowledge of the Lord as the waters cover the sea"
(Isa. 11:9).

I challenge you seriously to ask God if he wants you to
go. Perhaps he wants you to be a modern-day pioneer
who will change the eternal destiny of a nation that
presently sits in darkness. Be willing and obedient, trusting him since he always has your highest good in mind. If
he tells you to go, then go. He will take care of the details.
If he does not tell you to go then pray. Pray for specific
areas of the world, for the missionaries who are on
the frontlines there. Maybe he wants you to support
financially one of those that he *has* called to go.

GO FOR IT

Jesus said, "I have come to bring fire on the earth and
how I wish it were already kindled!" (Luke 12:49).
Evangelistic zeal is like a fire, and needs to be fed and
stoked continually to keep it burning. Human nature,
being what it is, tends towards coldness and indiffer-

ence to spiritual things, especially gospel work when it becomes uncomfortable. Re-read this book, study the scripture passages referred to so that your fires of zeal will continually be stoked by the consuming desire to see the Great Commission completed. Seek out, and get to know fellow Christians who are single-minded about missions and who can be examples for you of the lifestyle of evangelism. Read biographies of people God has greatly used in evangelism, and talk about evangelism, revival and missions with your Christian friends so that you encourage one another to love and good works (Heb. 10:24). Share with your friends those books and tapes that have moved you to a deeper commitment to God and his purposes. Above all, however, begin to witness where you are, remembering that you learn to witness by witnessing. It may be hard at first, but allow God the time to start in you a fire that will spread to those around.

Lastly, and most importantly, get close to Jesus. As we draw close to him he begins to rub off on us, his desires become our desires, his plans our plans. Spend time with him, spend days in secret fasting and prayer alone with him. If you diligently abide in him he has *promised* that you will bring forth fruit. Fruit that will remain (John 15:16). When the Lord returns may he find each one of us busy *bringing them back alive*.

Appendix A

Recommended Reading

LIFESTYLE EVANGELISM

Evangelism as a Lifestyle; Evangelism For Our Generation,
   Jim Petersen (Navpress). Two of the finest books on
   incorporating evangelism into your daily life.
Out of the Salt Shaker, Rebecca Pippert (IVP). An excellent
   book, from a woman's perspective, on the necessity of
   being "human" when sharing our faith. Provides
   a thorough examination of Jesus' methods of
   communicating the gospel.

STREET EVANGELISM

Arthur – A Pilgrim; Street University, Arthur Blessitt
   (Blessitt Publishing). Two books that are a guaranteed
   turn-on to evangelism by a man who, probably more
   than any other, has challenged the church to a lifestyle
   of evangelism.
Take Him to the Streets, Jonathon Gainsbrugh (Huntington
   House). Perhaps the most practical book available on
   street evangelism. It contains hundreds of helpful tips
   on street evangelism from a man who is dedicated to
   the task of sharing the gospel.

The Fisherman's Basket, Noel Gibson. This is the most complete book available on open-air ministry. A must for any would-be street preacher.

INSPIRATION FOR EVANGELISM

The Soul Winner, Charles Spurgeon (Eerdmans). Inspirational lectures on soul-winning by the "Prince of Preachers".

Revival Lectures, Charles Finney (Revell). A strong challenge to evangelism, revival and fervent prayer by America's foremost revivalist.

DISCIPLESHIP EVANGELISM

The Master Plan of Evangelism, Robert Coleman (Revell). A biblical examination of Jesus' strategy for world evangelism. Excellent reading.

The Lost Art of Disciple-Making, Leroy Eims (Navpress). Practical help and teaching on individual discipling.

MISSIONS

Is That Really You Lord?, Loren Cunningham (Kingsway). The exciting story of Youth With A Mission, with practical help on guidance and inspiration for missions.

On the Crest of the Wave, C. Peter Wagner (Revell). A concise, in-depth look at how the machinery of missions actually works.

Perspectives on the World Christian Movement, Ralph Winter, Steve Hawthorne (editors). An 800-page, 81-chapter examination of the biblical, historical, cultural, and strategic perspectives of world missions.

Appendix B

Sample tract

Presented on the following pages is a sample of a tract I have written and used in my evangelism. It is provided here to show the type of tract you could put together for your evangelism, or perhaps you may like to copy this one and use it. It is also provided as a model presentation of the gospel, one that you could adapt and use in your conversations with unbelievers.

The
FACTS
of
LIFE

FACT NO 1

GOD LOVES US AND WANTS TO GIVE US ETERNAL LIFE.

"For God so loved the world that he gave his only begotten Son, that whosoever would believe on him should not perish, but have everlasting life."   *(John 3:16)*

God loves each one of us personally. We are the highest of all his creation, being made in the image of God (Gen. 1:27). Each one of us is unique and special to him. Our Heavenly Father desires with all his heart that we would choose to live in his family for ever.

FACT NO 2

WE ARE SEPARATED FROM GOD BECAUSE OF OUR SINS.

"All have sinned and come short of the glory of God."   *(Romans 3:23)*

Every one of us has sinned (breaking God's law. 1 Jn. 3:4) which he has given us for our good (Deut. 6:24). Sin displeases God and hurts us and our fellow man. When we choose to live in sin, we are separating ourselves from God.

FACT NO 3

THE PENALTY FOR OUR SINS IS DEATH.

"Death passed upon all men because we have sinned." (Romans 5:12)
"The wages of sin is death." (Romans 6:23)

When we break man's law we must pay a penalty for our actions. In much the same way God, in his justice, has laid down a just penalty for our sins – spiritual death and eternal separation from him and his life.

FACT NO 4

JESUS CHRIST DIED, AND ROSE AGAIN, TO SAVE US FROM OUR SINS AND THE PENALTY OF SIN.

". . . Jesus, He will save his people from their sins." (Matthew 1:21)

Through Jesus' death on the cross, and resurrection, he promised to break the power that sin has over our lives if we would trust and obey him (Romans 6). He also took the penalty for our sins upon himself (Hebrews 2:9) and opened the door for us to be forgiven.

WHAT MUST I DO?

1. Repent: Make the choice to turn from all known sin.
   (Acts 3:19)
2. Believe: Trust in Jesus Christ, God's Son and His death on the cross for your sins. (1 Cor. 15:3)
3. Follow: Determine to follow Jesus as your Lord and Master, whatever the cost. (John 12:26)

My good friend: The purpose of this tract is to present to you as clearly as we can the gospel of Jesus Christ. Becoming a disciple of Jesus is not joining a religion or a philosophy, but beginning a relationship with God, as our Father. This is the relationship he created us to have – to be his children. Jesus has shown us his love by giving his life for us. Will you give your life to him?

STEPS TO CHRISTIAN GROWTH

1. Prayer – Talk to the Lord as your friend (Matthew 6:6).
2. Bible Study – God's Word is food for your soul.
3. Fellowship – Find a Bible-believing and Bible-teaching church or fellowship and attend regularly (Heb. 10:25).
4. Witness – Share your faith with others (Luke 24:46–48).